CONQUER THE CHAOS:
CBT WORKBOOK FOR TEENS

SIMPLE STRATEGIES TO TACKLE ANXIETY, SCHOOL STRESS, AND
SOCIAL AWKWARDNESS; PUT AN END TO DAILY STRUGGLES; AND
DESIGN THE TEEN LIFE YOU'VE ALWAYS DREAMED OF

CHELSEA CHAPMAN

CONTENTS

INTRODUCTION

For most people, reaching your teenage years marks the beginning of self-responsibility; this means that the support you get from your parents or guardians is transformed from one of utter dependence into nothing more than needing them to pay for your basic needs. More importantly, the start of teenage life also leads to severe consequences for common mistakes; the change is so abrupt that getting a bad grade on your homework may be treated like you have set your entire future on fire. Friends and many other people start changing as well; they all start responding to a set of standards on how we should act and treat each other—not that we are treating each other badly, but even kind gestures such as holding hands, hugging, or sharing some homemade lunch can be held to scrutiny during these difficult years.

I remember when my former classmate, Jimmy, brought cookies to school to share with the class as he always did every school year. While expecting the usual happy reactions that he usually received, he was surprised that everyone made fun of him for holding on to a childish tradition. When he went home, Jimmy yelled at his mother and asked her to never make him those cookies again. From that day forward, he went from being an outgoing and friendly guy to becoming a shy and socially withdrawn kid.

The changes that happen within our bodies are another challenge that comes with teenage life because, to some extent, it becomes awkward to even remotely talk about these changes with your parents or friends. The internet can help provide some information, but alone, it is usually not enough to get your mind off of your bodily changes, and this is when the feelings of loneliness creep in, especially if you feel like you don't have anyone to trust. The changes and challenges of teenage life can never be captured perfectly by research or case studies because, on some level, it will always be unique and personal— different for each individual. However, you must know that with the right tools, information, attitude, and healthy way of thinking, your teenage life can be as happy, joyful, and adventurous as you want it to be.

THE TEEN BRAIN

Borrowing the words of one of the greatest philosophers of all time, *"know thyself."* Aristotle identified the foundation and starting point for self-development. As a teenager, you are in the best position to get to know yourself—an opportunity missed by many adults. The best way to start getting to know yourself is by understanding how teen brains work. Information about the teen brain is a topic only found in specialized fields of study, formed recently due to information breakthroughs and aided by the use of technology such as MRI scans. The new findings discovered that the teenage brain is not simply a "miniature adult" brain as many professionals had thought, but sadly, many people—including teenagers themselves—are still holding on to this misconception. The fact is that the teen brain has certain parts that are not as developed as those found in the adult brain. So, if you have ever been confused to find yourself feeling happy in one moment and then feeling sad and miserable in the next, the straightforward answer is that this isn't your fault; it's because of the ongoing development and processes that are specific to the functioning of your teenage brain.

Understanding Its Growth and Development

Research has shown that the brain activities specific to teenagers are primarily meant to make teenagers adapt to changes in their environment. This is an evolutionary life characteristic that helps to give young people independence from their parents as they start to navigate the world by themselves.

This particular brain function is also responsible for your rapid ability to form new friendships—although, as a child, you were probably warned by your parents or guardians not to speak to strangers. On the other hand, this brain functionality also leaves you open to picking up dangerous and risky habits such as riding a bicycle without a helmet. Take note: This is not a lecture about your brain and your behavior, but it is background information that will provide a better understanding of your current brain situation, and you will need to know some of the basics, so pay close attention.

There is a part at the front of the brain called the *prefrontal cortex;* this is responsible for your ability to make plans, think about the consequences of your actions, and control yourself in intense situations. However, this part of the brain only gets strengthened in proportion to how you use it. We enter our teenage years heavily dependent on using the amygdala portions of our brains—which are located on the sides—to make decisions. This part of the brain is mostly made up of functions that stimulate emotions, instincts, and aggression. The prefrontal cortex helps us to exert control over how we express these base instincts, and it continues to develop up into our mid-twenties.

The process of moving away from using the amygdala towards the prefrontal cortex has been called "pruning." This simply means that as you use your prefrontal cortex and other parts of your brain more frequently, they will continue to get stronger, while the amygdala and the rest of the back of your brain will start becoming weaker as you use them less. However, as a result of the continuing, incomplete development of the front part of your brain, as well as a general lack of experience of the world, you will have a tendency to overthink various situations, like how bad a test at school may go, and sometimes, you may daydream on positive but distracting thoughts, like how nice it will be to see your crush at school. Then, as the thoughts intensify, you will be stimulated by the amygdala to feel a massive surge of emotions, such as fear or happiness in line with the nature of your thoughts. When you finally walk into that classroom and see that the questions are not as tough as you thought, you will be relaxed and will complete the test with no problem. But if you find the test to be as tough as you feared it would be, then it's possible for your fear to jump through the roof causing you to have a panic attack—which fortunately gets combated by your body's natural release of adrenaline that unfortunately makes it very difficult to sit still in a test scenario. Similarly, if you see your crush at school and they act exactly as you had pictured them while you were using your prefrontal cortex, your feeling of joy will be even higher; however, if they act in a way opposite to what you expected, then immediately, the amygdala will kick in and trigger strong feelings of disappointment. Thankfully, the skills contained within the pages of this book can help you manage the many changes your brain is going through.

Rapid Changes in Cognitive Abilities

Now that you have gained some insight into the structural layout of your brain and its specific functions that influence behavior, it is important to also know your cognitive capabilities and limitations so that you don't subject yourself to unnecessary stress. As mentioned earlier, your brain functions will push you into engaging with the world with a mindset and an emotional excitement that is open to various possibilities such as obtaining high achievements in your favorite sport, being liked by your friends, and so on. However, it is more than likely that the possibilities you are expecting will not match the results in reality. It's normal to feel a certain level of frustration or stress, but you should remember that this is part of the process of cognitive learning. Maybe, you will realize that you need to practice more in order to get a specific sports achievement award or that you need to be more kind or even to dress in a certain way to be liked or respected by others. This is where the second stage of cognitive skills kicks in, with questions: Do you care about your ideal possibilities becoming a reality so much that you would pay the price of practicing more or changing your behavior? In questioning your values and determining your personal boundaries, you will begin to use some form of critical thinking to determine the pros and cons of various choices.

As you start observing and taking note of what others have done to get the results you want to get, you must remember that you are performing the analytical steps that are part of critical thinking, and if you find that those people indeed took extra care in making effective behavioral choices, then you will know that you need to make the same effort as well. But if you find that they are more liked or have higher achievements in your favorite sport without any more effort than you are applying, you may feel a certain level of frustration or sadness, and another form of critical thinking that questions why certain people are treated differently from others will kick in. It is okay to feel a certain level of frustration after finding out the answers, but it is important to keep your emotions in check and not be carried away with thoughts that there is something wrong with you. Most of the time, the world simply needs a little more time to get used to our presence and efforts in a way that is comfortable to us. In the meantime, we can learn practical skills to help us navigate a world that expects adult levels of emotional regulation.

The Significance of Hormones

When you reach puberty—which starts between 9 and 10 years of age for girls and 10 to 12 years of age for boys—many brain and body activities are activated, including the high production of hormones; the substances that are produced to trigger certain processes within various bodily organs. These hormones, at these ages, prepare and prompt the body to start transforming and developing all organs that lead to sexual maturity.

It's normal to start feeling self-conscious and awkward at this stage. However, these feelings come into conflict with the brain activities that prompt you to be more socially active. This means that you will have massive surges of excitement to hang out with other teenagers and make friends, but you may also have a strong sense of caution against it. There are different types of hormones associated with the transformation of the body and brain activities during puberty, the main ones are testosterone and estrogen, which are found in both girls and boys but have different effects on each sex. For example, testosterone stimulates teenage boys to have low impulse control, leading to a high possibility of getting into physical fights; breaking things when excited, angry, or frustrated; or getting involved in risky activities like climbing on top of tall structures with little thought for their safety. This hormone also stimulates teens of both genders into a habit of thrill-seeking, which is also part of the process of self-discovery through the identification of things that bring pleasure to you and those that do not. Reward searching is also known to be related to the influence of testosterone; this is why the feelings of being underappreciated, unrecognized, and to some extent, unnoticed often affect many teenagers.

Another hormone that predominantly affects girls, and women in general, is estrogen, which is responsible for menstruation. It has been found that certain levels of estrogen have a direct relationship to feelings of depression. So, without the information on how your body is changing, it can be very scary, as a teenager, to realize that you have "unexplained" cycles of depression. Talking to someone about your mood swings— when they don't know the impact estrogen can have—might not provide any relief; as a matter of fact, it might even leave you feeling worse if, in response, you were left feeling invalidated. That's why it is so vital to understand your own mind-body connection.

SOCIETAL EXPECTATIONS VS REALITY

Teenagers are often caught in situations that force them to live a life that reflects the views that society has decided for them. However, these expectations are not based on realities that take into consideration the teenagers' personal backgrounds, capabilities, limitations, preferences, interests, or any number of a wide range of factors.

The Glossy World of Social Media

The impact of social media on teenagers has created a huge divide between what is real life and what is simply a highlight reel of perfectly packaged moments of happiness captured on Instagram or TikTok. It has become the norm to expect every teenager to not only have various social media accounts but also to be super active with posts that attract the attention of other social media users on the platform. Going to school without knowing the trending topics of the day can turn a teenager's entire school semester into a disaster. However, it should be noted that most social media posts and the content of people presenting exotic lifestyles don't reflect their everyday lives. Unfortunately, however, no matter how much you cognitively *know* this to be true, it can be very hard to *feel* the reality of this discrepancy. This makes it very common for many teenagers to feel like they are not living a life that is up to the standards of society. In general, posts that don't attract the expected level of attention and engagement, such as likes and positive comments, can make you feel like you're failing at life, and this can lead to self-loathing and low self-esteem among many other things. These social media conditions which drive the need to be super active on social media and post attention-grabbing content give many teenagers mixed feelings about the platforms that keep them constantly glued to the screens of their smartphones. For example, you may want to stay away from social media, but because of a term known as "FOMO," which means *fear of missing out,* you have been conditioned to constantly keep checking your social media platforms.

The Illusion of Perfection

The source of teenagers' (often overwhelming) desire for perfection often comes from social media, which has created the impression that everyone and anyone can look and dress like celebrities in the beauty and fashion industry. Back in the day, there was a general acceptance that certain looks and clothes were meant for a select few who were both rich and physically gifted. But today, most teenagers have found them-selves under the pressures of looking and dressing like Ryan Reynolds or Kim Kardashian. Additionally, even simple activi-ties such as singing in a school choir or playing sports can cause teenagers to feel judged by the standards of world-class profes-sionals. It is common for teenagers to feel like they are not good enough and give up on a particular skill that they could perfect over time. The reality is that people have different bodies, minds, talents, and finances, and therefore, it's not prac-tical for everyone to look the same way, wear the same types of clothes, or be good at the same things. There are a lot of expen-sive cosmetic or surgical procedures that teenagers cannot afford in order to look a certain way, and trying to live up to that standard leads to frustration and stress for many teenagers. In Chapter 5, we will take a deeper look at how to build and maintain your sense of self-worth within these impossible media standards.

Comparison and Its Detrimental Effects

Self-comparison has highly detrimental effects. Additionally, it has been made much worse by the use of social media as discussed above.

However, comparisons to popular and attractive people that we do not know on social media are not as traumatic and upsetting as comparisons with classmates and individuals that we know from around the neighborhood. While we can often challenge self-deprecating thoughts when comparing ourselves to someone who clearly has means beyond our own, it's easy to fall into the trap of assuming we ought to be able to keep up with the social media standards set by our friends.

Additionally, when people like your parents, siblings, friends, or others very close to you compare you against others, the negative effects of comparison are difficult to ignore. In the earlier example of a person getting good grades or a sports achievement award, a lack of evidence of any effort on their part can trigger jealousy, envy, and even hatred from other teenagers when they get compared to that person. You're not a bad person for having these negative responses, but they are influenced by the brain activities that have already been mentioned, and therefore, they can be lessened by the development of emotional regulation and self-fulfillment techniques. These will allow you to feel appreciated for the efforts you're making in living up to certain standards.

Peer Pressure in the Digital Age

Peer pressure through social media is very hard to avoid because the education and information on how to detect it is not as widely available as with direct physical contact and peer pressure. This makes it easier for teenagers to fall victim to social media influences that increase their exposure to risks which can lead them down a path of alcohol, drugs, or sexual abuse. Some teenagers who follow famous people—like musicians who make music videos showing explicit sexual contact, alcohol consumption, or drug usage content—can feel a need to start making social media posts that mirror those same activities to varying degrees. Then, these posts get viewed and shared by other teenagers and more posts get made. All of this can happen even if the musicians in question put a disclaimer at the end of the music video that they were not using real drugs or alcohol or actually making sexual contact when making the video. Despite the warning, a number of teenagers who did not see the video, nor its disclaimer—only the ensuing trends from their peers—will not know that the video activities are fake and will expose themselves to alcohol and drug abuse and, in some cases, sexually transmitted diseases through unprotected sex. Therefore, it is vital for every teenager to develop a strong understanding of their own core values and sense of self, which will aid in seeing through these trends and choosing healthy, helpful behaviors.

WHAT TO EXPECT FROM THIS BOOK

This book is not an overnight miracle to the various issues that you are going through, but you can rest assured that it will guide you through the necessary processes of dealing with many issues that are affecting a lot of teenagers all over the world. You are built with an amazing power and potential to have the teenage life that you want, and this can be achieved through the use of the cognitive behavioral therapy tools that will be outlined in this book.

Cognitive Behavioral Therapy

Cognitive behavioral therapy (CBT) is a process by which individuals address certain emotional and mental-related issues through the use of practical self-regulation skills, often taught during talking sessions with a psychiatrist or psychologist. The therapy is set up in a way that makes an individual identify certain ways of thinking and thoughts that lead to certain conditions such as stress, anxiety, and sleeping disorders, to name a few. Once the individual has identified these negative thoughts and patterns, it becomes easier for them to challenge self-criticism, choose effective ways of expressing emotions, and replace negative thoughts with positive ones that lead to a happier and more fulfilling life. The application of CBT is open to everyone, as it is extremely helpful for any form of stress, as well as more long-term anxiety and depression, and it can also be used for the treatment of complex mental issues such as schizophrenia and bipolar disorder among others. CBT is commonly used for teenagers because of the active and ever-changing internal and external conditions that usually leave them feeling stressed out, anxious, and uncomfortable in many situations.

With the CBT skills contained within these pages, you will be able to use and apply thinking processes that will greatly help you minimize the difficulties and challenges of your teenage life. So, let's get started!

CHAPTER 1

UNDERSTANDING ANXIETY—
IT'S NOT JUST "IN YOUR
HEAD"

There are a wide variety of anxiety disorders that range from social anxiety to post-traumatic stress disorders and many more. According to a report by the Anxiety and Depression Association of America, 31.9% of people between the ages of 13 and 18 are affected by some sort of anxiety disorder (*Anxiety Disorders—Facts & Statistics*, n.d.). Despite this, anxiety in teenagers only receives a small fraction of the focus that is given to adults. This is because of the myths and attitudes held by general members of society that simplify anxiety in teenagers. This often leaves a lot of teenagers uninformed about what anxiety really is, and those who have it have very limited opportunities to deal with it.

DEFINING ANXIETY

Knowing what anxiety really is will enable you to separate the common feelings that come with the sensation of having so-called "butterflies in your stomach" from the physical cues of a real anxiety attack such as the feeling of the hair on your arm standing straight up when you suddenly become the center of attention at a school or social event.

What It Is and Isn't

Anxiety is a sudden surge of fear and restlessness experienced when we encounter a certain situation; this is a normal reaction that prepares you to stay attentive and focused on the situation and effectively navigate through it. Once you have become used to the situation—usually with an acceptance that it is a reality and an establishment of what to do next—the fear and restless-ness will go away. However, some people experience these feel-ings much longer than normal, and the effect of this condition results in an anxiety disorder. The following examples will help you to have a deeper understanding of the various types of anxiety:

- **General anxiety disorder:** People with this type of anxiety disorder often have a wide range of fears and concerns about things happening to them that are unrelated to their current circumstances. For example, they may worry that they will be a bad parent before they even consider having a child. The sources of these concerns and fears are often unclear and tend to sneak up on them in very weird places, like in a business meeting.

- **Panic attacks:** Anxiety often has what are called *triggers* that are responsible for making someone feel uneasy or anxious. Triggers can be certain smells, sounds, or places that can give someone a panic attack and make them extremely restless to the point of shaking like they are faced with a terrifying creature or sweating as if they just finished running very fast on a hot summer day.

- **Specific phobias:** People with this anxiety disorder tend to have an extremely uneasy reaction towards the sight or sound of certain things such as a specific animal. It is common for people with phobias to know that they have them; however, it is their lack of control over their feelings of fear when they encounter their specific phobia that can make this condition debilitating.

- **Selective mutism:** This is a type of anxiety mostly common in children, who find it hard to speak when they are in certain places or circumstances. Despite the misleading usage of the term "selective," people with mutism have little to no control over this loss of verbal ability.

- **Social anxiety disorder:** This is a type of anxiety that makes people overly self-conscious when they are in a social setting. Their concerns and fears can range from wondering if their outfit is appropriate to assuming that their friends secretly hate them and are just being polite.

Physical, Emotional, and Cognitive Signs

The extent to which anxiety affects our bodies, feelings, and behaviors is so diverse that in some instances, the anxiety may be so specific to an individual that it cannot be placed in any of the main categories. The following are some of the most common physical, emotional, and cognitive signs of anxiety:

- **Chest pains:** It is common for most people to think a person is having a heart attack when they see the person clench their chest in pain, only to realize that it was an anxiety attack after calling emergency health providers to the scene.
- **Muscle tension:** Another physical sign of anxiety comes from the lack of ability to relax one's muscles while sleeping or sitting alone in a quiet place. It is common for many anxious people to experience pain in certain areas of their bodies such as their shoulders, back, or neck.
- **Stomach issues:** Other common symptoms of anxiety may include constipation, flatulence, and bloating, as well as other gastrointestinal problems. Some people throw up when a plane is taking off due to the anxiety related to the rapid changes of elevation.
- **Fear of rejection:** This is an emotional sign of anxiety that can present itself even in simple situations like asking to sit next to someone at school and worrying that they might say no. An anxious person who becomes overwhelmed by this fear often starts to get sad as if they have already been denied the request in

reality. This causes people with anxiety to avoid making any requests.

- **Feeling irritated:** Another sign is an inability to maintain your cool when involved in a situation that is deemed to be inappropriate but that should be ignored. For example, uncontrollable laughter or the sounds of a person chewing can make someone with anxiety lash out uncontrollably or leave the place while fuming in anger.
- **Trying too hard to be perfect:** This is a cognitive anxiety sign that makes a person obsess over getting something done according to their perfect standards.
- **Avoiding certain places and people:** Another sign of anxiety that impacts a person's cognitive functioning is when they start avoiding certain people or places that remind them of a phobia they have or a traumatic experience they went through.

Recognizing When It Becomes Pathological

It still may not be clear how to tell the difference between everyday concerns and an anxiety disorder, especially if none of the previously mentioned signs have occurred. As a teenager, knowing the fact that you have a super active brain and imagination will help you to notice if your anxiety has gone too far; this may be the case if you find yourself worrying about the following issues:

- failing your tests and finals or not being able to reach certain sports achievements *way* before the actual day of attempting to succeed
- diseases or violent attacks from home intruders or vicious animals
- disasters, wars, and apocalyptical events

The sooner you speak to someone about these issues, the better because delays can lead to one or all of the following situations:

- difficulties in handling school matters effectively
- trouble establishing healthy social connections
- feelings of self-loathing
- suicidal thoughts

Early anxiety intervention measures are usually effective during your teenage years when the conditions are just developing. Having professional help will enable you to have a teenage life that is enjoyable and avoid carrying anxiety into the later years of your life where it can become extremely complicated to treat.

The Spectrum of Anxiety Disorder

It is common for anxiety disorders to blend or develop into other mental health problems such as clinical depression and many others. This is why it is important that you pay attention to the physical, emotional, and cognitive symptoms that have been highlighted in this chapter and seek medical attention right away if you see a pattern emerging.

The Story of Mike Allen

Mike Allen is a 14-year-old boy who likes to explore extraterrestrial concepts that he reads about and watches on TV. Last year, when he was 13, Mike forced himself to stay awake all night long because he suddenly believed that aliens may come from other planets and kidnap children at night. Then, Mike started being late for school and would sometimes have difficulty concentrating in class as a result of the exhaustion from his lack of sleep. Soon after, he was failing several classes and finding it hard to hang out with his friends. The school assigned him a specialist who determined that Mike had an anxiety disorder and referred him to a mental health professional. It was recommended that his immediate treatment be psychotherapy sessions that lasted 16 weeks. Mike was able to overcome his anxiety problem and has continued to follow his passion for exploring the concept of life on other planets, with an ultimate goal of studying astrobiology in college. Like Mike, you too can prepare for a successful future by addressing any anxious thoughts this early in your life.

THE ROOT CAUSES OF ANXIETY

There are a wide variety of causes of anxiety that can be traced to various roots according to research and data reports that have been made by experts. Below, we will discuss several of these possible causes.

Biological Roots

As highlighted in the introduction of this book, teenage brains heavily operate from the amygdala region, which comprises feelings and emotions, rather than from the prefrontal cortex, which gives us cognitive, logical reasoning. As we experience anxiety—such as a sudden concern that you will have to give a presentation next week—the prefrontal cortex aims to regulate and reduce the anxiety build-up with logical thoughts that you are always given a few weeks' notice of any presentation assignment and will do your presentation in the same manner as you have seen other people do them. In people with an anxiety disorder, the surge of worries coming from the amygdala overwhelms the prefrontal cortex's abilities to manage them and calm the body and mind, which consequently leads to anxiety attacks.

The Role of Genetics

There has been a lot of supporting evidence through research that some genes associated with anxiety and mental illnesses can be passed down from parents to children. Additionally, severe traumatic moments may shift the genetic layout of an individual to create a new survival skill similar to the thousands of years of genetic shifts that have given humans today our general, inherent survival instincts. However, this may be categorized as a hereditary vulnerability to anxiety when the activated gene is passed on to a child. Additionally, there is a general opinion that the rise of anxiety in children and teenagers is likely through the role of genetics as opposed to coming from extreme experiences; nonetheless, medical treatment is the key to resolving the issue.

Hormonal Changes in Teens

The surge of hormones in teenagers' bodies through this wild process of transformation into adulthood can also be responsible for anxiety. The mood swings, lack of sleep, low energy levels, and physical changes that teenagers go through can cause great stress about their overall well-being, discomfort being around others, low performance at school, and other developmental difficulties. Also, the need for excitement, rewards, and thrilling activities caused by these raging hormones may not turn out as expected, creating concerns about uncertainties to the point of being highly anxious.

Fight-or-Flight Response

The fight-or-flight response is a survival reaction that kicks in when we come face to face with imminent danger like a bully at school charging at us. The fight-or-flight response triggers brain activities and chemical reactions in our bodies to become focused on the threat and make an assessment of whether to fight or run. However, some people experience the fight-or-flight response even when there is no danger at all. It may not be clear to the individual why they find themselves feeling like they are ready to fight or run when everything around them seems so calm and peaceful, but this may point to a dysfunction in the brain and body chemistry processes.

Environmental Triggers

This is the most underrated cause of anxiety, but its impact is often as huge as the other causes that have been outlined. Environmental or social factors that make us uncomfortable—like noises, pollution, bad weather, discrimination, bad relationships, and many others—may lead to anxiety disorders. The reason why most people tend to overlook environmental factors is because of how we have become conditioned to tolerate things that we know are below standards; however, their impact is subtle and may lead to anxieties that require clinical treatment.

Stressful Life Events

As a teenager, the number of stressful events and situations that you may be going through is so diverse and numerous—like the lack of control over the changes in your body and mind, social conflicts from the clash of personal views and opinions with those of others, and even the news reports of injustices from remote countries; these can all induce stress. Unlike adults—who have many coping advantages for handling stress like a fully developed prefrontal cortex and the money to afford all kinds of stress regulation tools and products—teenagers often have to deal with stress using limited capacities which may lead to the development of anxiety conditions. However, the lack of coping mechanisms may itself add to the stress with additional concerns about being independent and whether you are ever going to have a prolonged stress-free moment.

ADDRESSING MYTHS

Myths and misconceptions about anxiety can be a much greater danger to society than anxiety itself. These myths have greatly contributed to the reasons why anxiety is on the rise in children and teenagers, and more efforts have to be applied towards breaking this cycle of myths being passed from one generation to another, across cultures and among the general population.

Common Myths

The following are the most common myths:

- Anxiety is not a mental health sickness.
- Anxiety is just a life event that goes away on its own.
- When you have anxiety, you should stay away from stressful situations.
- Anxiety disorders are rare.
- You may faint if you have a panic attack.
- Using a paper bag while hyperventilating will help ease your breathing.
- Shyness is also anxiety.
- Everyone has anxiety.
- Using medication is the only way of dealing with anxiety.

Let's address a few of these, and more, in detail.

"It's Just a Phase"

It is common for many people—generally parents and other adults—to dismiss the anxiety challenges that teenagers are going through as just a phase of life that will go away. This often leads to many anxieties not getting addressed in their early stages, and then, they intensify in adulthood when the symptoms have become so severe that the individual is unable to carry out the daily tasks of managing their lives. It is sad that adequate support and recognition of anxiety-related issues in teenagers is so rare that a person's anxiety must reach such high levels before it is given the attention it needs. By changing the culture and cycle of calling anxiety "a phase," parents and society will be able to provide help to a lot of teenagers and give them various powerful coping mechanisms.

"Everyone Feels This Way"

The impact of this idea of everyone having some form of anxiety makes teenagers who are very much aware of their particular anxiety issue afraid to talk about their struggles and challenges for fear of being invalidated and told that they are making a mountain out of a molehill. Those who manifest anxiety signs can easily be stigmatized, bullied, and ridiculed because of a misconception that they are being weak or merely seeking attention. This leads to the isolation of people with anxiety, which further intensifies their challenges and can be a factor in the development of further anxiety disorders and mental health issues.

"Just Stop Overthinking"

This is a common phrase that many people with anxiety are told, and it can greatly lead to frustration, stress, and irritability, which makes anxiety worse. People who use this phrase a lot lack a general understanding of anxiety and further contribute to the discouragement of many people with anxiety from seeking professional help. It is true that some anxiety can be treated with various changes in how we think, but just telling someone to merely stop overthinking is like asking someone to stop a certain reflex action from happening. What people should do is encourage and support those with anxiety to seek a diagnosis and get professional support.

"You're Too Young To Be Stressed"

Adults often turn to teenagers and tell them they need to reach adulthood and start working, dealing with mortgages or rent, or have children of their own before they can truly know what stress really feels like. This often leads to issues and challenges of stress associated with teenagers being taken lightly or not considered at all. It should be noted that there isn't much difference between the environmental issues that cause stress in adults and in teenagers. For example, job-related issues, like meeting deadlines, are similar to the pressures of doing homework or assignments placed on teenagers. In fact, this stress may impact teenagers to a larger degree, as they do not have the freedom or societal respect to make their own choices or stand up to authority figures who ask too much of them. This shows a very important point that experiences and feelings of stress and anxiety are not related to age but apply to all people.

THINKING ABOUT ANXIETY IN PRACTICAL TERMS

As you navigate your teenage years with an understanding of the differences between anxiety and everyday concerns, you will not fall prey to the misconceptions that many people have about anxiety. With the knowledge about the common types of anxiety—such as social anxiety disorder and general anxiety disorder—you will be able to know when treatment is necessary to overcome the issue; additionally, you will also be able to use your knowledge of the general causes to narrow down the cause of your anxiety. Understanding the need for and importance of seeking professional help as early as possible will enable you to have peace of mind; this is because medical research and advancements in psychotherapy have shown how anxiety works and how to treat it.

One-third of teenagers deal with anxiety, and talking openly about it with friends is most likely going to help those affected to feel comfortable talking about their feelings and struggles as well. Talking about the issues you are dealing with will create a support structure around you that will bring relief and help you cope with stress. So, do you still feel like your teenage years could turn out to be the worst experience? Regardless of your answer, the application of the CBT practices in the following chapters will not only help you through the challenges of your teenage years but also give you lifelong enriching experiences. Next, you will learn about what CBT is and how it works.

CHAPTER 2
INTRODUCTION TO CBT—YOUR TOOLBOX TO CONQUERING CHAOS

What if you had the power to rewire your thoughts? We are all aware of the difficulties that we go through when we attempt not to think about certain things, especially when these thoughts make us uncomfortable physically, emotionally, and mentally. The struggle with negative thoughts has been so severe in many people that they have ended up a danger to themselves or others. With the use of cognitive behavioral therapy (CBT), you can detect, change, and lessen the impact of any thoughts that cause negative feelings, attitudes, or behaviors.

THE BASICS OF CBT

CBT is a psychotherapeutic treatment that can be used for various mental illnesses and anxiety disorders; these disorders cause certain emotional responses as a result of certain ways of thinking or behavioral patterns. CBT aims to break down these emotional responses by changing or removing the thoughts or behaviors a person has that keep making these emotions happen. In certain instances where a person has multiple anxieties, the treatment involves changing or altering the ways of thinking and behavioral patterns simultaneously to achieve the best results.

The origins of CBT can be traced back about 70 years to the 1950s when B.F. Skinner and Joseph Wolpe partly introduced this form of therapy. Skinner and Wolpe's research established theories that changing behavioral patterns was a key step toward the management of certain emotions and various aspects of cognition or understanding of objects or people. This led to a movement that established what is known as *behavioral therapy*.

Over time, the use of behavioral therapy saw its evolution due to the research work of psychologists such as Albert Ellis and Aaron T. Beck, and this brought about the development of *cognitive* psychotherapy. This new type of therapy was built on evidence that changing certain ways of reasoning led to changes in emotions and, consequently, behavioral patterns. Cognitive therapy can be thought of as the reverse of behavioral therapy; however, the two therapies were both effective and had been supplemented by one another frequently. Over time, the two therapies eventually merged and became what is now known as cognitive behavioral therapy (CBT). It should be noted that CBT has been constantly evolving by including specific psychotherapeutic tools designed to target and handle specific anxiety disorders and other mental illnesses to achieve the best treatment results. Keep in mind that the parent treatment therapies of CBT—cognitive therapy and behavioral therapy—are still being used individually for very specific and rare anxieties; however, the use of CBT is the most common.

CBT can be applied in many various ways depending on the patient's anxiety disorder and their therapeutic needs according to the evidence of extensive studies and research. There are two main categories of treatment used in CBT therapy: exposure therapy and cognitive therapy. Understanding how each category works will give you knowledge of the applications of CBT for the treatment of specific anxiety disorders. Take note that no matter what category of CBT is being used for a particular anxiety treatment, it will usually involve the following components:

- analyzing the conditions of a moment
- evaluating and reforming thinking structures
- improving emotional processing
- considering general senses and feelings
- recognizing and readjusting behaviors

Exposure Therapy

Exposure therapy is a category of CBT treatments based on how emotions process information from a cognitive way of thinking, interpreting information such as objects, sounds, impulses, and thoughts; reacting to them, causing an emotional response; and then, resulting in a certain behavior. It should be noted that there is usually a mismatch between the reality of things and the information that the cognitive way of thinking processes. This affects emotions, causing people to worry, be fearful, or panic. For example, cognitively, the sight of a poisonous snake crawling nearby will make you process, interpret, and conclude, at light speed, that you are in a dangerous situation, setting off a fear response that prompts you to run for safety. However, a fear of snakes can generate the same cognitive interpretation that leads to the same emotional process, even when there is no snake anywhere in the person's environment. With exposure therapy, this condition can be mitigated and overcome through three types of treatment: imaginative, in vivo, and interoceptive. All three types of exposure treatments involve the activation and restructuring of the cognitive way of thinking that causes emotional responses that aren't based on reality, showing them that even in a feared scenario reality often contradicts their negative cognition.

Cognitive Therapy

Cognitive therapy is based on the relationships between thoughts, feelings, and behaviors—widely known as a tri-part model by many mental health practitioners. Cognitive therapy involves the targeting of certain ways of thinking that affect a person's feelings and subsequently their behaviors. For example, a person who has thoughts of being unworthy will always feel lonely and yet will avoid any situations or people that could possibly prove their intrinsic worth. The cognitive therapy treatment of a person with such thoughts will involve sessions with a therapist who targets this unhealthy self-judgment and helps to create a new sense of self that will replace the unhealthy one.

ADAPTATIONS FOR VARIOUS AGE GROUPS

Responses to CBT treatment will often vary among children or teenagers and adults due to the differences in brain activity. This is similar to how prescription drugs for common illnesses often have recommended doses that depend on a patient's age. The following variations of CBT have been developed to make the treatment more specific to teenagers:

- **Cognition behavior connectivity:** This process involves an extensive analysis of how negative thoughts cause unhealthy physical responses and behaviors, as well as how positive thoughts stimulate healthy alternatives.
- **Detecting unhealthy thoughts:** This involves teaching teenagers how to identify the unhealthy thoughts responsible for certain behaviors such as how a fear of public speaking can lead to a person avoiding group activities.
- **Behavioral changing:** This is a process of challenging negative behaviors such as avoiding homework out of fear of failure, and replacing it with a more healthy or effective behavior. This could look like starting with the subjects you're good at to build your confidence before tackling difficult assignments or saving a certain TV show to only watch after completing your homework, which will act as external motivation.
- **Talking sessions with a therapist:** This provides a safe place where teenagers can openly speak about their emotions and work towards a specific goal, like

becoming comfortable with having a different body than the ones popular on social media.

- **Developmental consideration:** This modifies CBT to use a language style and a system that is more suited to teenagers.
- **The participation of family:** Where possible, this involves the use of family bonds to accelerate a treatment goal.
- **Emotional control:** Lessons are given on the techniques for controlling emotions—for example, using grounding techniques when angry to self-regulate and avoid saying or doing something regrettable.

How CBT Changed Sheila's General Anxiety Disorder

Sheila is an 18-year-old who often had concerns and fears about the end of the world. This negatively affected her goals of completing her senior year of high school and going to a university. She found that she couldn't bring herself to care about anything because of her thoughts that the world was coming to an end. The situation got worse when she realized that her behavior and her thinking were negatively affecting her 10-year-old sister. Moved by the love she had for her sister, Sheila decided to start attending CBT sessions with the goal of changing her behavior. Her commitment to the treatment was driven by the need to become the best big sister, but she quickly came to the realization that she needed this change for her own sake too. Over the course of her CBT sessions, Sheila also realized just how beautiful and wonderful living in the moment really is. Her experience with CBT has led her to live her life focused on doing the things she loves—among them, playing with her sister and paying zero attention to things that don't matter.

HOW CBT WORKS

To get a clearer picture of how CBT works, you should become familiar with how the following anxieties are treated with CBT therapy.

Post-Traumatic Stress Disorder (PTSD)

This type of anxiety disorder comes from thoughts surrounding severe traumatic experiences that produced thoughts that led to certain emotions and behaviors. CBT changes the present thoughts surrounding this past situation. The first step will involve asking you to write down the reasons why you think the traumatic event happened and how it changed your outlook and view of the world. By safely exposing you to the traumatic event through your writing, this treatment allows you to look at the event from different perspectives, which will help to reduce your associated fears or concerns related to the event. By repeating this process over and over during different sessions, the therapist will challenge your beliefs of why you think the traumatic event happened to you. A shift in that belief will also reinforce the new perspectives of thinking about the event, giving you the ability to control your response to difficult memories and choose thoughts that will enable you to manage the associated fears and concerns that you used to have.

Obsessive Compulsive Disorder (OCD)

When you are diagnosed with OCD, CBT will be used to challenge unhealthy cognitive beliefs that are created by unrealistic opinions of situations, people, or yourself. The process will involve sessions that will assess the importance you place on having these thoughts—like the example of Mike Allen, it is common for so many people to think of UFOs and aliens, and possibly their alleged sinister plans for people. However, most people do not place such importance on having these thoughts that it keeps them awake all night. Likewise, very few people feel compelled to perform specific behavioral rituals, like turning the light on and off five times, to compensate for these fears. The therapeutic sessions for this condition also include guidance and practical methods to resist judging yourself harshly as a bad person for having such negative thoughts about things or people. As you attend more CBT sessions or when applying the concepts alone, you will begin to feel more relaxed, confident in your ability to challenge these thoughts whenever they pop into your head, and able to control behavioral impulses, like the way Mike cut down on drinking energy drinks to stay up at night.

Panic Disorders

CBT will help you to identify thoughts and beliefs that are generated from a general feeling of discomfort like being in a crowded place or stuck in an elevator. These thoughts cause a wave of feelings that make you feel tense, find it hard to breathe, and experience many other physical symptoms that usually only happen when a person is confronted with imminent danger. You should be aware that feeling uncomfortable is sometimes a normal part of everyone's life, but regularly feeling panicked is not. However, panic is not itself a reason for despair, and eventually, you will be able to prevent the thoughts that trigger you whenever you feel uncomfortable. Over time, the prevention of such thoughts will become automatic.

Generalized Anxiety Disorder (GAD)

The CBT approach for treating generalized anxiety disorder will involve you challenging the thoughts that are responsible for your anxiety. For example, Sheila, who had extreme worries and fears about the end of the world, challenged those thoughts with the fact that most cultures throughout human history have been passing on information from one generation to another about the impending end of the world, and yet, it has never come. Once she was able to use this challenge to gain some distance from her anxious thinking, Sheila was able to recognize that her fears about the end of the world were actually associated with her concern for her family's well-being, especially that of her little sister. Additional sessions later on enabled her to develop techniques for reassuring herself that her family was safe. Over time, she was able to realize the peace of the environment she lived in that greatly contradicted the thoughts that made her anxious. Whenever these old thoughts would pop up, she would challenge them with the thinking that an impending apocalypse is a human idea as old as time but that does not make it true, and she was also able to visualize and enjoy the peace of her current environment. Over time, her negative thoughts have become less frequent, to the point that they no longer cause her to worry or be afraid in the way she used to be.

Social Anxiety Disorder

CBT treatment of social anxiety will involve having you identify any negative perceptions that you have about yourself, causing stress and concerns that people will look at you in the same way. The first approach will involve helping you identify the thoughts that prompt you to criticize yourself and how you can disrupt those patterns. Once you have recognized these thoughts, you will break them up and see what you can change through your thoughts and what may necessitate a behavioral approach. For example, if the negative thoughts about yourself surround the fact that you easily get angry and social events have the potential to make you overreact, then you will be exposed to therapies that will build your ability to maintain self-control in anger-triggering situations. On the other hand, if the negative perception has anything to do with something that you can't change—like not coming from a family with as much money as that of your classmates' families—CBT will help you to come to terms with and manage the hardship as much as possible by challenging the perception with a new way of thinking and reasoning. This may, for example, mean reminding yourself that you are not responsible for your family's money and equally, your classmates are not responsible for the money their families have, and that wealth is not equivalent to worth. With further sessions, you will be exposed to other valuable personal qualities that you have, like kindness, creativity, or any other skills and talents. This challenges the self-perception that reinforces social anxiety.

The Thought-Feeling-Behavior Triangle

Our thoughts, feelings, and behaviors are interconnected, and knowing how the three work together in this triangle will increase your understanding of how CBT works. Thoughts make up the top part of the triangle, then emotions and behaviors are at the two bottom, foundational parts. As a teenager, you are more connected to the base of the triangle—connected to the areas of your brain that don't take as long to develop. That is why you are more aware of your feelings and what you do than of your thoughts.

However, it is important to know that your thoughts have a much more direct impact on your emotions than on your behavior, and likewise, your behavior also has a more direct impact on your emotions than your thoughts. So, during your teenage life and into your early twenties, you will be more aware of your emotions than your thoughts or behaviors. This is where CBT comes in by drawing your attention to your thoughts and behaviors in order for you to control how you feel. For example, you may be invited to a friend's birthday party but can't attend because you have the flu. This will cause you to feel sad for your friend who needs you in this situation, and then, the sadness will make you feel guilty, which in turn makes you think that you are a bad person for missing your friend's birthday party and causes another emotion such as feeling shame. Here, you can see how an initial stimulus can cause emotions and thoughts that can get stuck in a negative feedback loop without the interruption of CBT skills.

Additionally, without adequate coping mechanisms, the shame you feel can make you try to ignore your thoughts and feelings by forcing yourself to attend the party, but certain behaviors, like sneezing, that reflect your flu will make you feel worried and generate thoughts that you will make your friends sick as well; this will cause behavior that will make you appear anxious to be around the people at the party. You may realize that you now feel much worse than you felt when you were at home because, in this situation, your feelings will confirm that you were justified in not wanting to attend the party, which will make you feel even more guilty with additional thoughts that you are a bad person for putting your friends at risk with your flu; this will further strengthen the anxiety to socialize at the party. CBT tools and applications teach you how to prevent this type of cycle from happening by helping you recognize your thoughts, emotions, and behaviors and how they impact one another and then changing them accordingly in a way that leaves you feeling great about yourself, doing things because you want to and controlling any negative thoughts.

GETTING STARTED WITH CBT

Getting started with CBT is very easy, especially now that you have an overview of how it works; all you need to do is design your approach to using CBT in the following ways.

Setting Goals

Starting out with clear goals is the best way to make CBT work for you, even CBT sessions with a therapist involve outlining goals for what you want to accomplish. Your goals can be reducing the stress that comes from assignments in class or improving how you feel when things do not turn out exactly how you wanted them to be; you could aim to decrease your general concerns about how people think of you at school; you can set any target that you think might be helpful for focusing your use of practical coping mechanisms. It is recommended that you use a goal-setting model called *SMART,* with each letter expanded as follows:

- **Specific:** Your goals have to be specified with a clear definition of what you want to work on—for example, to reduce your worries over the safety of your family.
- **Measurable:** You should be able to measure your progress because CBT is a process-based therapy and does not involve one-time fixes. One way you can measure your goals is by identifying which thoughts or behaviors cause you stress and tracking how often they occur or become debilitating.
- **Achievable:** You have to be real with yourself, and don't promise yourself results that are beyond your abilities to deliver; an unattainable goal would sound like this: "to stop all worries from entering my mind again," or "to think I will never fail a test."

- **Relevant:** Your goals must be compatible with the proven applications of CBT. There's no point setting a goal to become a champion skateboarder; unfortunately, no amount of emotional regulation will magically gift you those talents.
- **Time-bound:** Your goals must have timelines in which you have set to achieve them.

"I want to reduce how often I give into anxiety-related impulses by at least 10% this month" is one example of a CBT SMART goal.

Preparing Yourself Before You Get Started

CBT is such an exciting concept that many people who discover it get really overexcited to have their lives transformed and dive into this treatment unprepared. However, you must approach the use of CBT with the following mindset:

- **Mental readiness:** You must understand that the therapy will involve coming face to face with stressful, fearful, and worrying situations, even though the natural tendency is to avoid them. The first step of using CBT effectively begins when you reject the urge to avoid these thoughts, feelings and behaviors and acknowledge that they are a natural part of your life. This is the only way you will gain the power to make the necessary changes to certain thinking patterns, emotions, and behaviors that make your teenage life difficult.

- **Embracing failures and setbacks as learning opportunities:** You must remember to exercise patience and try not to get frustrated when you find that your goals have not turned out exactly as you wanted them to be. Take some time to review how you are applying the CBT concepts, and try again.
- **Keep an open mind to the possibilities of CBT:** Yes, there are other treatments and therapies out there such as prescription drugs that help to bring down stress levels in some people. You may begin to think that, maybe, CBT is just additional hard work in your life, but think of CBT like maintenance on a sports car. This is what prevents a breakdown and the need for that "roadside assistance" of medication—which does not truly cure emotional hardship but instead is usually more like the tow truck to help you get to the point of engaging with therapy anyway.
- **Maintain a support structure:** It is important to tell your parents or the friends who really support you about your goals with CBT; take their feedback seriously while maintaining your commitment to applying the concepts of CBT.

Alex's Diary Entries

Alex was a 16-year-old boy who was too afraid to talk with anyone about his feelings about wetting the bed. He was so ashamed that he didn't even feel comfortable talking to a professional therapist because he was afraid of being judged; instead, he wrote his feelings in his diary. After learning about

CBT at school and how he could apply the concepts to himself, he decided to give it a try. After several weeks of trying, he was able to understand that having a negative opinion of himself, because he wet the bed, was making him feel ashamed. He realized that he was placing so much importance on wetting the bed that he didn't give himself credit for the great things he did, like helping his single mother with chores around the house. A few weeks later, Alex felt more reassured that wetting the bed was his personal and private business because he did not share his bed with the people around him. He also realized that by putting a towel down, he could relieve some of his anxiety about possibly wetting the bed, which allowed him to get a better night's sleep even when he did wet himself. His thoughts of wetting the bed disappeared, and as he continued to grow older, he realized he was no longer wetting the bed. Many years later, when Alex was an adult, his mother found his diary in his room after he had moved out of the house; with nostalgic laughter and a tear in her eye, she confessed that she had always known about him wetting the bed but never mentioned it to him because she didn't think it was anything to be ashamed of. With the clarity of hindsight, she wished that one or both of them had said something so that Alex could have had access to support through such a difficult time.

There are so many factors that can contribute to having a stressful time during your teen years, but developing a support network can hugely lessen the impact of these stressors. This is particularly important when it comes to enduring one of the most universal teen nightmares—the topic of our next chapter: school.

CHAPTER 3
THE LABYRINTH OF SCHOOL STRESS—NAVIGATING ACADEMICS

I t's often not easy to get adults to understand how stressful school life can be. Most of the time, teenage school stress is only recognized in terms of tests, assignments, and presentations; however, it comes from various sources—sometimes much more severely. A Yale University survey revealed that 80% of high school students identified school stress as the number one feeling they have each day of their lives (Senior-Year Stress, n.d.). It has also been found that the stress management tools that are available to many high schoolers are too limited and narrow in addressing the various causes of school-related stress that teenagers themselves point to. To be more specific, stress management systems in schools are often designed only for management of the stress that comes from tests and assignments. This situation has led to many high schoolers giving up on the ideas of using school-related stress management programs. Thankfully, a lot of schools are finally recognizing the need for widening their stress management programs, and they are starting to make students aware of this change. However, it might take some time for the results of this movement to become effective enough, and maybe, you can't afford to wait that long; so, take matters into your own hands and use CBT to reduce your stress levels during middle and high school.

UNDERSTANDING ACADEMIC PRESSURE

The information explosion that has happened in the last 20 years—due to increased technological breakthroughs that have made communication and traveling across huge distances very affordable—has produced new information that high schoolers are expected to know. Curricula are changed every day, with new discoveries and innovations being made, and each semester, high schoolers have to keep up with these changes if they are to remain successful in keeping their grades up. This is much worse than the effect of FOMO with social media, that deals more with current social needs; academic pressures have a double-sided effect because of the fears and the current need to stay in school combined with the pressure of getting into college.

High-Stake Tests and Grades

The increase in the awareness of the importance of education and its availability through many private and public schools has led many parents, and society in general, to have very high expectations. Often, these expectations do not reflect a high schooler's individual circumstances or capacity to live up to the grades that they are expected to get. What's even more interesting is how most people who expect high schoolers to have exceptional academic performances provide little to no support, like helping with homework. The entire system of expectations has even led to the development of curricula and college acceptance criteria that are based on these expectations —to the point that all high schoolers, regardless of their aspirations for higher education, feel its impact. This should answer your question of why you find yourself so scared of tests. You frequently fear failure, and you fear disappointing everybody because you have been asked to live up to impossible societal expectations. So, what can you do about this? Obviously, you can't get angry and argue with everybody for having these expectations of you; instead, you must challenge yourself to break free from these expectations with a new way of thinking. You can start by recognizing that education is important, and then understanding your strengths and weaknesses, which will help you to effectively use your energy to get the grades you want. Use SMART goals—as covered in the previous chapter— to set up a strategy and work your way slowly toward improving your grades without having to deal with the fears and concerns that come from unrealistic expectations.

Homework Overload

As if school tests and assignments are not enough to cause high levels of stress, daily homework adds to the pressure and may leave you with no time to rest and get your energy back. This can leave you unable to handle not just school work effectively but also other activities as well. This overload may cause you to feel utterly exhausted and take a toll on your body and mind so severely that it may reduce your ability to concentrate or focus on anything. This may cause negative thoughts to develop and cause stress and frustration to shoot up, leading to emotional, mental, and even physical breakdowns.

Expectations Vs Reality

It is possible to get caught up with societal expectations and move away from what you really want. People may expect you to perform exceptionally well in a subject because your mom or dad works in the industry that it is related to. For example, if one of your parents is a doctor, you may be pressured into believing that you should be able to do well in subjects related to the field of medical professionals—even when your own intellectual skills lean towards subjects related to business, music, or any other field. This may turn you away from focusing on subjects that you are really good at, preventing you from planning which college programs would be most suitable for you. This mismatch of expectations and reality will make you pressure yourself into trying to be perfect in a subject that you have little interest in and giving little time and attention to the subjects that you love.

College Admissions and Future Prospects

Many teens dream of going to college one day and studying whatever it is they want, but why does this excitement turn into fear and worry when high schoolers are in their senior year? For some people who have always known that they will engage in higher education, the dread of college can even start in junior high. Whichever the case, the experience of looking forward to independence does not always turn out as well as many thought it might. This is also associated with the pressures that come from the requirements of getting into college, as most of the time, meeting these requirements is intimidating. Besides, many high schoolers are also aware that the tuition fees required for the colleges they would like to attend will put them at a disadvantage.

BEYOND ACADEMICS: EXTRACURRICULARS AND SOCIAL DYNAMICS

The challenges of school are usually easy for teenagers to talk about among themselves However, there are other struggles that are too personal to be discussed with their friends or family.

Extracurricular Commitments

These are activities that are not directly school-related in the way that tests, assignments, varsity sports activities, or school club programs are. These activities are supposed to give you a space away from the school system where you can explore your passions on a self-guided level. However, these activities are often included in a school curriculum as a way of making you develop effective methods of exploring your interests. This may complicate the nature of what these activities were intended for and instead lead to additional pressures that are based on performance rather than experience and progress. It can be difficult to explain to friends and family that the activity they think of as your "fun time" is actually a source of stress.

Friendship Dramas and Peer Pressure

During your teenage years, school is also a place where friendships are being held to certain standards that come as a result of societal expectations. Your opinions, and those of your peers during your teenage years are most likely going to be affected by emotions, and the experience of being confronted by anyone who thinks differently than you will feel like an attack; additionally, opposing opinions from your friends may seem like a betrayal, to the point that you may never want to have anything to do with a friend that comes to you with a contradicting opinion. You may also be surprised to find that a friend may get angry at you and say mean things when you have certain feelings about a movie or TV show that are different from theirs. In order to avoid confrontations and in the interest of preserving your friendships, you may feel under pressure to have the same opinions as those of your friends, and this can cause you to make yourself feel very uncomfortable. Additionally, having the same opinions may not be enough for some of your friends, especially those who have difficulty with respecting others' boundaries; they will ask that you prove your opinion to them by doing something that will convince them. And because you are a nice person who cares about how your friends feel, not doing what they ask you may make you feel like you are a bad person, but giving into people-pleasing urges, in the end, contributes to making the whole friendship unhealthy.

Popularity Contests

Being popular is not a bad thing; however, it's also not necessarily a good thing. Feeling the need to become popular is associated with the evolutionary need to expand your social engagement options. In past eras, this allowed groups with more people to have access to more resources including the safety of extra watch guards. During your teenage years, you are exploring who you are through other people's eyes as well, and this can make your need to be popular feel very important because popularity provides a sense of safety from the judgment of others during this vulnerable self-discovery.

However, what we perceive as popularity is sometimes infamy and is certainly nothing to be strived for. In fact, aiming to mirror the actions of a "popular" person can even be damaging. For example, a person's popularity can have nothing to do with anything that is life-building, healthy, or respectable, but if you feel left out because you think that no one is noticing you and you start to copy the person or people who are popular without realizing the consequences of doing what they do, you may engage in impulsive, reckless, or simply callous behavior to "get ahead." You may even try to get into a popularity contest with these people and go to the extremes of unhealthy behaviors leaving you surprised that you end up with the opposite of what you wanted in the first place—not being liked and being avoided at all costs. Be who you are, and do the things you love to the best of your abilities; and as was mentioned earlier, in the introduction of this book, sometimes, people just need a little more time to notice and appreciate who you are.

Seeking Genuine Connections

Finding genuine connections is a very hard thing to do, regardless of your age, but for teenagers, the process is often met with disappointments because of a lack of experience with how to tell that you have indeed made a genuine connection with someone. Additionally, people can also change or move away, making this need even more intense and leading to feelings of loneliness, which can turn into concerns about whether you are ever going to make a genuine connection. Genuine connections are necessary for our overall well-being because of the assurance they bring that someone will make the choice to support and understand you, not because they are your parent or sibling but because they like you. Being liked in this manner also gives people a general confirmation that they are right for somebody. Again, exercise patience knowing that the path to building genuine connections is not a straightforward one; people make mistakes. So, strive to be a genuine person first, and never give up on who you are. Then, genuine connections will happen as well.

Finding Balance

Finding balance can mean additional work on top of all these pressures that have been explained so far; however, you may use the following tips to establish a balance:

- **Create a calendar:** Start at the beginning of the month, and write down all of the important upcoming activities such as tests, assignments, and time for fun—

such as playing video games or going to the mall. Mark your calendar with the specific times of the day when you will be doing these activities. After creating the calendar, create a system of checking it once or twice after a period of time; it is always best that you check it at night before you go to sleep so that you know what to expect the next day, and check it again in the morning on the actual day so that you can mentally prepare for the tasks ahead.

- **Set reminders:** The best way to do this is to use your smartphone apps, or even better, sync your calendar with reminder apps that will give you a notification about an upcoming activity.

- **Personalize your schedule:** There are some activities that can be considered as set in stone—such as the day you do the house chores, the scheduling of laboratory experiments, or any other regular or externally timetabled task—and also those that are up to you to arrange, like studying, doing your homework, or taking the family dog for a walk. Arrange the flexible activities according to the functionalities of your body and mind. For example, if you find that you wake up early, like 4 a.m., then you can set your study time at this hour. Similarly, fun activities like going to the mall and playing video games can be arranged during the times when you normally feel more sluggish.

- **Utilizing tools:** It can be helpful to use tools like apps that measure your progress and planners that enable you to outline your goals. Make the most out of what is available to make your activities preplanned in a way that will make them easy to handle when the day and time comes.

- **Prioritizing:** There are times when your calendar or tools are not as effective as you had hoped or you underestimate the amount of time needed to study for a test or to complete a task. Then, make adjustments to your calendar and focus on handling what is most important first, and later doing the less important tasks in the most practical and logical order.

- **Make time to have fun and relax:** This is also a necessary part of development as a teenager. Through fun and relaxing activities, you get to recharge your energy and are able to be more effective when handling serious activities.

- **Find support:** Create a support group with friends; support can come in the form of encouragement, help in understanding a confusing or difficult topic, or many more actions.

- **Be realistic and flexible:** Having a calendar of activities is just one way of organizing and managing yourself and your tasks before the day and time comes to do them, but sometimes, you may need to skip one or two things to attend to an emergency or something with a higher priority. For example, you may be unable to study at a certain time because you feel tired and need to sleep, so don't allow negative thoughts about changing your calendar to make you feel bad.

CBT TECHNIQUES FOR SCHOOL-RELATED STRESS

Using CBT techniques to manage school stress should never be rushed to the point that it also starts to feel like another assignment or test you must pass. Changing your thought patterns is a process, so apply CBT concepts in a way that puts you at ease throughout the process. If you try to force yourself to change your thoughts, the flow of the process will break, and the experience will become just another chore.

Practice Mindfulness

The use of mindfulness has shown to be an effective way of calming someone's stress and negative energy levels stemming from unhealthy thoughts. Mindfulness can work for anyone regardless of their level of stress. Use the following steps to apply mindfulness:

- **When you wake up:** It is important to wake up by reflecting on how you are feeling and acknowledging the thoughts that you have. For example, you may be feeling bad that you did not do your homework last night and have thoughts that this is going to affect the grade you get for the class or affect the rest of your school year. What's vital here is to simply observe these thoughts and emotions rather than jumping straight into problem-solving mode. Giving yourself the emotional space and safety to notice these patterns is the first step to overcoming them.

- **Breathing exercises:** Breathing exercises are meant to make you more aware of your thoughts and improve your brain activities with an increased supply of oxygen. While you focus on a distressing thought—like the example above, that your grade for a class may be affected because of a missed homework assignment— breathe in and out very deeply and slowly. Then, turn your attention solely to your breath, noticing the rise and fall of your chest and abdomen and feeling the flow of air in through your nose and out through your mouth. As you focus on your breath and body, you will notice physical tension being released from your muscles. In turn, this prompts a reduction in your worries, to the point that the thought will become less and less stressful. More thoughts will come, including possible solutions to the source of the distressing thought, until eventually, you will have full control of the thought and its associated feelings and be able to replace them with positive thoughts and feelings.

- **Focusing on your senses:** This is the best way of being in the moment. You may be at a party but worrying that your friends at school are not going to like something you want to tell them. Thoughts about how each friend will react may even take over your mind, generating feelings as if a prolonged confrontation and conflict were currently happening. A friend at the party may give you a nudge for the millionth time, asking you if you are okay, but obviously, your answer may make them doubt it because they can already tell that your mind is somewhere else. Focusing on your senses is the most effective way of being present whenever your mind begins to wander. You can do this by applying what is called *the 5-4-3-2-1 rule*—a grounding technique based on our five basic senses: Direct your attention to five things you see, four things you hear, three things you smell, two things you feel with your skin—like clothes on your body or shoes on your feet—and one thing you taste. This will work for you in any situation, even in your classroom during a test, allowing you to relax and focus.

Setting Boundaries and Learning to Say No

As you navigate through your teenage life, your empathetic abilities are going to be very high and lead you to exercise great sympathy for others. This is a good thing, but we can't solve all of someone's problems; every teenager knows this, but have you ever wondered why and how you found yourself committed to an activity that is beyond your limits to deliver— for example, promising to play video games with your friend a few minutes before your curfew? This is because you place more priority on how they will feel if you say no than on your own limitations. However, if you don't know how to say no, when the time comes for you to deliver on your promise or you're in the middle of an activity that you agreed to be a part of, you become anxious that it is too much for you to handle and pull back, leading to more disappointed feelings than you and the other person would have felt if you had just said no in the first place. This does not mean you are a bad person if you have done this before, but you must treat this experience as a learning opportunity. It is okay to say no sometimes. Before saying yes to a request, take your time and check your schedule, your energy levels, and your nonnegotiable commitments.

Prioritizing Activities

Learning to prioritize a selection of tasks is not always going to be a straightforward thing to do, but it might help to use the following strategy:

- **Write down all your important tasks:** Write down all of the tasks that you need or want to complete, and then, separate them into daily, weekly, and monthly tasks based on their importance and urgency.
- **Order your tasks according to the consequences of failing to do them:** This should be done with the consideration of what will happen and who it will affect if you do not do a task.
- **Stick to a schedule:** Before taking on a new task, it is vital to consider the order in which you have already placed your other tasks and why. You can't just skip a scheduled task because a friend has asked you to go to the mall with them for an exciting last-minute clearance sale.
- **Tackle the most difficult and time-demanding tasks first:** While you still have a lot of energy, it is best to handle the tasks that are the most difficult and work your way down to the easy ones. This process will also encourage and motivate you as a result of the positive

thoughts that you have already handled the difficult part.

- **Handle one task at a time:** It is tempting to try and do everything at once, but this will cause more stress and make your overall performance less successful than if you handled the tasks one at a time.
- **Be realistic:** You must consider your limitations, and try not to push yourself into completing a task that needs a lot of time, work, or more than a single attempt to finish.
- **Work with others:** Create a task management support system with your friends and family, working together always creates an environment that makes the work easier.

Having a solid task management system and a supportive network of friends and family makes handling any difficult emotions more manageable. But what happens when friends themselves become a source of hardship? Don't worry; as you'll see in the next chapter, CBT is always there for you!

CHAPTER 4
THE DOUBLE-EDGED SWORD
OF FRIENDSHIP

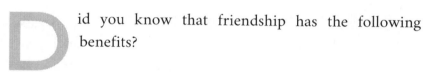id you know that friendship has the following benefits?

- reduces anxiety and depression
- increases happiness and optimism
- builds your emotional management skills
- increases the quality of your cognitive functions
- enables you to understand how others are feeling
- builds your confidence to take risks and trust others

Your teenage years are the best time to build friendships and connect with people at school and in your community. But you should know that unfortunately, some supposed "friendships" can be so full of toxicity that they make you feel that friendships, as a whole, have nothing more to offer than trouble and more stress. Worse still, unstable or toxic friendships can lead you to believe that there is something "wrong" with you, that you're not "trying hard enough," or even that you "deserve" the disrespect that you're receiving. This chapter will guide you on how to make and maintain friendships that create positive results and how to avoid and overcome the influences that can lead you to or keep you in unhealthy friendships.

THE POWER OF FRIENDSHIP

Extensive research and studies by experts have provided a mountain of evidence showing that people who have strong friendships during their teenage years have consistently better mental and physical health. Additionally, it has also been observed that many adults who have maintained the friendships they created in their teenage years through experiences such as birthdays, graduations, and more had much better mental and physical health than their isolated peers. If you have not yet found friendships that you believe will last, don't start worrying that you will develop mental or physical health issues! Take note that friendship, in general, promotes health and well-being, regardless of age; that's one reason why you see so many older people joining retirement groups—it's *literally* part of their healthcare. So, why not include reaching out to others as part of your self-care routine?

Finding a Place of Belonging

A solid, supportive community comes with a wide range of positive impacts:

- **Psychological benefits:** As a teen, friendships can help you navigate the difficulties that come from school-related issues, body changes, fluctuating brain activities, societal pressures, and family dramas. Because your peers are going through many of the same stresses, they can relate to and support you in a much different way than your parents or siblings.

- **Great mental health and self-esteem:** Having supportive, communicative friends means that you not only have the reassurance that you are not alone in your difficulties—since they also tell you about their worries and everyday stress—but also the empowerment and confidence boost of them telling you small things like how great you look when you are feeling anxious before going out or recognizing your skills and abilities. This will help your self-esteem and reduce any feelings and thoughts that can give you anxiety or mental health issues.

- **Support:** Friends will always be there to give you support in times of need; this support can be demonstrated in the form of assurance that you will do well the next time you have to take a test or a gentle hug after the loss of a beloved pet. The best kind of support is mutual, occurring through a shared activity that leads to equal beneficial outcomes for all people involved. For example, if you and your friends want to learn how to play a new video game, you will support each other by sharing tips and encouragement during the process. Likewise, empathetically sharing your own experiences of a type of hardship that your friend is currently experiencing can help them open up to you while also providing you with an emotional outlet.

The Dynamics of Friendship

Friendship is a very interesting concept that has attracted the interest of a lot of scholars and researchers who aim to understand its role in human interactions and how it shapes or influences experience. There is a pattern that friendship follows among different age groups of people. Do you remember how, when you were younger, your desired outcomes for friendship were much different? Like most little kids, you probably liked hanging out with other children because of the way their toys, the food in their home, and many things in their environment made you feel. But once you started maturing past this stage, your needs for friendships were expanded to include the following areas:

- receiving affection that satisfies the need to be accepted
- enjoying good company that accepts and respects your ways of thinking about how you should be treated and behave
- advice that helps you through the realization that your decisions have a direct impact on your well-being

- validation of your interests through your friends' participation
- support for your hopes and dreams through your friends' reassuring attitudes and encouragement
- the safety to conversationally explore your changing ideas on romance

Cliques, Groups, and Personal Identity

As the transition from childhood to mature teenage friendships occurs, a lot of things happen as you go about subconsciously or consciously trying to get the most out of the friendships you make. It is never an easy process to develop friendships that consistently satisfy your diverse needs as a teenager because you and your peers are all growing and changing so rapidly that it's easy for you to outpace each other in maturity in different aspects of life. For example, you may make friends who validate your interests but do not yet have the emotional capacity to actively listen and give you advice or those who support your feelings about your romantic relationships but struggle to engage with your hopeful conversations about the future. This will lead you to search for people to fill the gap that is not being satisfied by your current friendships; however, you must consider and understand that your peers are also faced with the same situation as you.

Often, this constant fluctuation in identity, and thus friendship stability, creates a large level of emotional vulnerability and fear of judgment or abandonment, and when a lot of teenagers are all in one place—like a school or a community club—it can lead to the creation of cliques and groups. Each clique or group you belong to is shaped by a main interest that is vital to everyone, like an interest in shopping, but each individual in the group will have behaviors or feelings that contradict your other needs for friendship. For example, some of the people in your group will put you in situations that push your boundaries or disrespect your limitations. This creates a conflict between who you are as an individual and the functioning of the group, leading you to toggle between bad and good times every time you are with your clique.

It's okay to have been taken in by this pattern. Your teen years are a difficult time, and it's understandable to have made choices to make them easier. The important thing to remember is that you still need people that you can be 100% yourself with. Thankfully, CBT can help you develop these friendships and set and maintain boundaries within cliques. But before we discuss these practicalities, it's important to fully understand the necessity of implementing such coping skills.

THE SHADOWS OF PEER PRESSURE

When conflicts of interest among friends in a group develop, each one of you will try to defend who you are and prove that you "deserve" to be seen by others as a real member of the group. Subtle confrontations will take place; these often take the form of pressuring you to do something that almost everyone in the group is comfortable with; at times, this could mean feeling under pressure to put yourself in an uncomfortable position where you must face your fears or even contradict yourself to be respected and acknowledged as you would be in a true friendship. This is what peer pressure is all about, and instead of producing the benefits of friendship that were outlined at the beginning of this chapter, it causes stressful situations and leads to habits that make you feel bad about yourself.

You must not be too hard on yourself whenever you find that you have to give in to peer pressure. Without the practical knowledge that CBT provides, it can be extremely difficult to figure out how to navigate these types of challenges when trying to create meaningful friendships. Keep in mind that most of the time, your friends won't know that they are actually pressuring you into doing something you don't want to do; they too have probably not been taught emotional regulation, and therefore, they are likely to be easily swept up in trying to remain a member of the clique and addressing their own insecurities. It can be helpful to understand the types of peer pressure so that you can recognize them when making friends:

- **Spoken peer pressure**: This happens when a friend asks or tells you to do something.
- **Unspoken peer pressure**: This is an underlying sense that you *should* do something, generally suggested through the behavior of friends. When you experience unspoken peer pressure, you will often be left with a nagging urge to act in the same manner as your friends as a way of validating them and their behavior.
- **Direct peer pressure:** This is more activity-driven behavior when you are with your friends, and it can be manifested either through spoken or unspoken peer

pressure. For example, being handed alcohol to do a toast with on New Year's Eve despite neither you nor your friends being legally permitted to drink alcohol.

- **Indirect peer pressure:** This involves ways of thinking that challenge or urge you to do something when you are by yourself—for example, the negative comment sections of social media sites can normalize cyberbullying or hearing a rumor can make you want to spread it.

- **Negative peer pressure:** This is the peer pressure we always hear about, where you are directly or indirectly urged to do something that does not align with who you are and what you believe.

- **Positive peer pressure:** Not all peer pressure is bad, certain behavioral influences and things that friends ask you to do can be considered positive peer pressure. For example, if you and your friends often discuss your grades, it will provide motivation to improve, add value to your overall performance at school, and help you overcome certain fears.

How Richard Struggled With Peer Pressure

Richard is a 14-year-old boy who comes from a wonderful family that provides him with more than enough food, trendy clothes, cool gadgets, and plenty of video games. However, just like every other teenager, his family could not buy him friends. He struggled to connect with people until he started hanging out with a group of boys who did not seem to feel the pressures of their teenage years. They were always laughing and talking about all the trouble they would get into. One day, they invited Richard to go out with them to the mall. Excited, Richard went along, but he then discovered that they were all into shoplifting.

After the day was over, they would brag about what each one of them had stolen, and when they turned to Richard, they talked about how sorry they felt for him that he lacked the "courage" or the "skills" that they had. Every time Richard would go home, he would feel torn between what they were saying about him and his strong moral beliefs and need for safety. As the friendship went on, things got worse because the boys in the group would make fun of him or say things that made him feel uncomfortable around them. But they were the only friends he had. So, to make them stop talking about him, he decided to steal something with them one day. His actions changed everything. His friends were more proud than he ever thought they could be just from him doing the same things they did. He went home that day feeling really good about himself, but when he was alone in his room, away from all of the positive comments they gave him, reality kicked in and he felt bad about what he had done. He realized that he was better off with them making fun of him and that no amount of praise was worth this risk to his future.

Yet, the next day, his guilt and fear had faded, and since he hadn't worked to develop his emotional permanence, he wanted to experience that rush of approval from his friends again. So, Richard joined them and stole more stuff; once again, their approval came but not with as much gusto as the day before, and he immediately started feeling bad while he was with them. Over time, the approval from his friends became less and less, and they again began to pressure him into worse behavior. His personal feelings about what he was doing had increased to the point that he was starting to hate himself.

It is hard to think about how many young people could better their circumstances, not just during their teen years but for life, if only they knew how to avoid such pitfalls.

FORTIFYING YOURSELF AGAINST NEGATIVE INFLUENCES

There are methods you can use to reduce the effects of negative influences from certain friendships that you will create in school or your neighborhood. The following methods have proven to be the most practical and effective.

Building Assertiveness and Resilience

Being assertive is a good thing, but it is important to understand where assertion crosses the line to aggression; there are ways in which you should communicate your needs and boundaries so that you do not come off as inconsiderate or intimidating. Try to remember that most of your friends are still going through their own process of self-discovery and might not have the capacity to communicate equally as effectively, but by sticking to your core values and extending compassion in your own communication, you can help develop new norms that will keep your friendship strong.

- **Know that people have different experiences that shape their beliefs and activities:** You should know that you will come across people who do things differently from you; listen to them with an open mind, and try to understand their point of view.
- **Patiently explain why you can't do certain things:** There is a good chance that you will eventually give in to the pressure to do something if you don't explicitly explain that you won't. So, telling your friends why you can't do something allows them to see the logic behind your decision and not take it personally.
- **Keep in mind that your reasons for not doing something will never make sense to everybody:** There will be times when friends will disagree with or make fun of you for not being part of an activity, but you should know that you are allowed to make your own decisions and have your own limits. Stay true to yourself; you know what you should or shouldn't do.

CBT Techniques for Peer Pressure

There is so much you can do to protect yourself from negative issues, but some things will always find their way into your mind, affecting your feelings and behavior. For example, the hundreds of posts that you see on social media can increase the possibility of you giving in to negative influences. CBT techniques can help you to utilize positive thoughts that make you feel great about yourself. If you see a post saying that those people who missed the party last weekend are lame, mentally challenge it with the knowledge that there are other ways of being cool and having fun.

Cultivating Genuine Connections

It may not be enough to tell some types of friends that you can't be a part of their activity for personal reasons, and some friends may not know when enough is enough when making fun of your reasons for not doing something. At this point, you will be able to determine that the friendship is not healthy and you probably should distance yourself from it. Genuine friends respect one another. It is not okay to joke about each others' personal preferences because genuine friends care about your boundaries as much as they care about their own. Having a lot of friends is nice, but the best way of maintaining quality friendships is by having a small, close circle. The fewer friends you have, the more time and energy you will have to spend on building a genuine and long-lasting connection.

CHAPTER 5
THE DIGITAL DILEMMA—
SOCIAL MEDIA, SELF-IMAGE,
AND SELF-WORTH

D o you know that teenagers spend about seven hours per day looking at the screens of their smartphones, computers, and TVs? Six hours of this screen time involves activities that require an active connection to the internet. That's over a third of your waking hours! This has brought a lot of opportunities to have instant access to videos, pictures, and information from people anywhere in the world. Despite this impressive human development, the internet has brought many challenges to a lot of people in terms of their emotional and mental well-being.

NAVIGATING THE DIGITAL LANDSCAPE

As exciting as digital landscapes such as YouTube, TikTok, Snapchat, and Google can be, it's important to pay attention to the changes to the platforms that influence people's behaviors, feelings, and attitudes.

The Rise of Social Media

When first introduced to the public, most of these digital spaces were used for connecting with people you knew and keeping up with their various activities and events such as birthdays, graduations, and weddings. People largely posted content in an effort to make their friends feel close to them. Then, the ideas of online marketing and influencing others through these platforms began, and the focus on post engagements, such as likes and reshares, became the measure of validation and approval of what was posted. Over time, many people started holding themselves to the standards of marketing establishments, leading to a desire—that morphed into a need—for social media attention.

Then, the marathon of posting content simply to get likes began; social media platforms like Instagram quickly introduced photo and video editing tools like filters and sound effects not only to help users polish their content but also to keep them on the platforms. This has resulted in a large leap in competitive mindsets and new forms of bullying both through and about a person's social media. Gossip over the number of likes someone's post received has become part of the new norm. Some people completely withdraw from social media due to fear of being judged. Additionally, our societal dependence on social media has become so normalized that those people without a social media presence have become the target of all sorts of uncomfortable and negative criticism. This has led to many people keeping a low-activity social media presence that does not draw any attention to themselves.

Comparison Culture

Social media—in addition to other societal factors—has created a culture of comparisons. Before posting, many people now consider the norms and opinions of other people who make similar posts and the kind of attention they receive. However, this comparison also focuses on people's (perceived) quality of life. Social media posts of delicious-looking food can make a person surviving on hot dogs and mac 'n' cheese feel awful about themself. Likewise, the glitzy highlight reel of social media can make many of us feel inadequate when it comes to our clothes, fashion, dating, and many other general real-life activities.

Online Validation and Mental Health

The biggest issue with overvaluing external validation is that it diminishes your desire—and eventually, ability—to validate yourself. Soon after joining social media, a teen's self-validation of how they look before they go to school can become irrelevant, replaced with taking a photo and attracting a considerable number of likes from friends. The process of doing this has contributed to the rise of stress in many people. Consider the fact that organizations and celebrities have a high number of paid marketers and public image builders who spend a lot of hours creating messages and photos that will generate positive responses from their followers, but many people using social media today try to accomplish all this by themselves in a very short period of time. This has contributed to an increase in mental health issues that show up through various symptoms such as trouble sleeping.

The Impact of Social Media on Mark's Mental Health

When Mark got a smartphone on his 13th birthday, he quickly installed all of the popular social media apps. He had an artistic talent for making photos more visually appealing using Photoshop and other editing software. Soon after installing the social media apps, he started Photoshopping his pictures onto different backgrounds of a range of exotic places around the world, making it look like he had really traveled there. This made him popular with many social media users both globally and from his school. It was a very good feeling; maintaining his popularity meant posting more types of edited photos. But deep inside, he felt like a fraud and started hating the attention he was receiving at school. Over time, he developed social anxiety due to the fear that people would find out that he had never been to any of the places that had made him so popular. Eventually, he started withdrawing from both online and physical social engagements—to the point that he started missing school, as well. Thankfully, his family intervened and booked some CBT sessions for him.

THE DISTORTION OF SELF-IMAGE

Social media has contributed to many people holding an unhealthy self-image in many ways, such as being judgmental of their own physical appearance, personal beliefs, social statuses, and many other areas of their personal lives. Knowing the details of how this occurs is a key step toward challenging the thoughts that urge you to keep up with impossible standards.

The Filtered Reality

Artificial intelligence (AI) photo and video filters as well as editing software have become much more advanced in recent years, and people who don't know or understand how these filters work are more likely to fall victim to their trickery. Eventually, the pressure of living up to this unrealistic social-media-altered beauty standard can cause body dysmorphia—an obsessive, negative, and untrue view of how you look. When your behavior is more aligned with social media's filtered posts than with real life, people may begin to confront you about how you actually look, which can reinforce the belief that you need the filter to look acceptable. This may lead to a desire to reduce your real-life social interactions because you prefer your online image. Unfortunately, this is how some teenagers live their lives: going to school wearing clothes to disguise themselves yet being so popular on social media—while deep down inside, longing for physical interactions with friends. If you feel this way, CBT can help you to build your trust in, and acceptance of, both yourself and others, guiding you through developing healthy relationships.

Cyberbullying

Cyberbullying is another social media problem that has become common in many modern cultures around the world. Many teenagers and adults are not aware of the different forms of cyberbullying, and this makes it harder for them to even know how to deal with them. Here are the 10 most common forms of cyberbullying that you should know about:

- **Exclusion:** This is a type of cyberbullying where a person is intentionally left out of a social media post or group. This could look like a post saying, "the cool kids are in my class," with everyone but you tagged or people discussing conversations from a group chat that you are not a part of in front of you.
- **Harassment:** This is a more direct method of cyberbullying through the use of insults or threats to make you think less about yourself. For example, you may post a photo of yourself having a weekend dinner with your family and then receive a never-ending onslaught of messages about how awful the food looks and that you should be ashamed that no one in your family knows how to cook.
- **Outing:** This type of cyberbullying involves sharing your embarrassing or private moments on social media for all to see. For example, you may have accidentally slipped in the cafeteria, and someone captured the incident on video and shared it all over social media. The video can even be customized with text, sounds, or objects to intensify the humiliating effect of the post.

- **Cyberstalking:** Social media stalking works exactly the same way that in-person stalking works, which is through someone constantly checking up on you and gathering personal information. Social media stalkers may appear like friendly social media followers, and they may even tell you about posts you made several months ago including the exact times you made them. This can make you feel awkward, anxious, or afraid that the person knows too much about you, but it can also feel incredibly validating; be careful not to feed into a stalker's habits or encourage this kind of behavior.

- **Fraping:** This is the intentional act of another person logging into your social media account and making inappropriate posts as a way of ruining your social media image or embarrassing you.

- **Fake profiles:** This is a type of cyberbullying that can be used to make you feel like your friends don't like you. For example, fake profiles of the people that you usually hang out with can be created with their exact profile pictures. Then, these fake profiles can all start making harassing posts targeted at you; by the time you realize that they are fake profiles, the damage may already be done emotionally and mentally. Without emotional regulation skills, it can be easy to get very upset or become consumed by anger, and this may lead you to impulsively use your profile to fight back and make angry posts about your friends, damaging your relationships.

- **Dissing:** Just as we hear about in popular music, this is a form of harassment that comes with the added insult and humiliation of publicly entertaining other people.
- **Trickery:** This is a type of cyberbullying that takes advantage of the need for genuine connections and friendships among many social media users. The cyberbully usually tricks the person into revealing personal and private information which is then used to make embarrassing posts.
- **Trolling:** This is the intentional use of bad language or insulting posts about a person's image, personal beliefs, or political convictions to make them angry enough to respond in an emotional state. And because the words we use or the way we react when we are angry can reflect badly on our personalities and characters, the bully puts a focus on and highlights this reaction as a way of making you look bad to others.
- **Catfishing:** This is the use of someone's personal information to create a social media profile that can be used to contact people for various deceitful reasons such as carrying out a scam or manipulating someone into developing a romantic attachment.

How Patricia Embraced Her Natural Beauty

Patricia is a 15-year-old girl who would hang out with friends who were highly addicted to adding filters to photos they took together before posting them on social media. Patricia found that a final decision on which filters to use would take them several hours, and this time was cutting into her other important activities like going to dance practice and doing homework. She was stuck with the difficult decision of whether to prioritize her academic and extracurricular needs or the emotional need to post a perfect picture on social media and gain self-esteem-boosting validation. She later realized that her need for validation didn't have to be satisfied externally. When she participated in a self-esteem-building program for young girls, she learned that some messages of the cosmetic industry and social media filters were responsible for self-esteem issues in girls and women. She had to make some difficult steps towards building her self-esteem, one of which involved posting her photos without filters; initially, this had a negative effect on some of the friendships she had, but she had already learned that she felt better when she prioritized her own values. Eventually, she noticed that some of her friends had also started posting their photos without filters. Soon afterward, she reunited with her old friends and had deep conversations about other things, which actually strengthened their bonds in the long run.

BUILDING RESILIENCE IN THE DIGITAL AGE

It's clear that the digital age is here to stay; this is because the benefits greatly outweigh the costs and risks of this innovation. However, more education and awareness on how to use the internet safely is needed. In the meantime, you will need to build resilience to protect yourself from the negative effects of the digital age.

Digital Detox Strategies

Most people say that they only use social media when they simply want to pass the time or take a break and relax from schoolwork. But all of us can sometimes have difficulty putting the phone down. Nevertheless, taking a break from social media can greatly reduce the possibility of being negatively impacted by it. Take note that the first few days of living without social media can make you feel lost, like a part of you is missing. But remember that it is only uncomfortable because it is unfamiliar.

Engage in pleasant, distracting activities when you are not busy. In particular, any activity that gets you outside and surrounded by nature will help. This is because being around greenery naturally improves our body's production of dopamine—the happiness and reward hormone that social media withdrawal can cause you to crave.

Enhancing Real-World Connections

Try to maintain a steady balance between your social media presence and your engagement in the real world. One of the best ways of achieving this is by taking part in scheduled activities with other people. You can find out about camping trips being organized in your area or participating in organized voluntary exercises like going to feed the homeless, walking dogs at a pet shelter, or going door to door to talk about environmental awareness programs. Use the following CBT techniques to help you further enhance your real-world connections:

- **Cognitive restructuring:** This is the process of correcting any mistaken beliefs that you hold about digital life, such as that people without an active social media presence are boring or that you aren't capable of being witty in real life without the use of memes.
- **Behavioral experiments:** Practice leaving your phone at home, and take notes of how you feel and think about this change of behavior. Then, use relaxation exercises when you get anxious that you left your phone at home. Replace the thoughts that tell you that you should always have your phone with you with an understanding that you can do and feel very well even when you aren't connected to the digital world. Use the 5-4-3-2-1 exercise to stay mindfully present and not mentally and emotionally drift to your phone at home.

Next, you will learn about how to build emotional resilience to protect yourself not just from the negative effects of social media but also from many other situations in life.

CHAPTER 6
BUILDING EMOTIONAL RESILIENCE

With all the many different influences on your emotions that have been mentioned in this book so far, the need to build emotional resilience is a task that can clearly be defined as a major teenage goal. It is important to approach the idea of building emotional resilience with an understanding that like any strength, your resilience will only grow with use but also that the right techniques can ensure rapid emotional resilience growth.

UNDERSTANDING EMOTIONAL RESILIENCE

Emotional resilience is your ability to function in a rational way when faced with upsetting or challenging emotions such as anger, heartbreak, disappointment, embarrassment, or stress. This is knowing and feeling these emotions and yet continuing to do your homework, complete your chores, and go to school safe in the knowledge that you can handle it all.

Emotional resilience is important because you may find that you can't keep up with the demands of life. Additionally, it will maintain and strengthen your relationships, as it helps you withstand disagreements or emotional challenges. Since people generally only remember the actions you take, emotional resilience empowers you to leave a better impression on people and build stronger relationships through enriching your impulse control. Having emotional resilience also provides some of the following key benefits:

- handling situations with a sense of maturity through the use of analytical skills and logical actions
- knowing whether you can really handle a situation and asking for help if you can't
- managing stress more effectively
- no longer judging yourself harshly when a difficult situation arises
- the ability to use preventive measures like having habits that minimize instances of emotional turmoil
- the capacity to resist self-destructive behaviors

Additionally, you can start building your emotional resilience by following the *7Cs model*:

- **Confidence:** Confidence is a strong belief in your own skills, knowledge, and experiences. While it is difficult to know the difference between confidence and cockiness, the first place you can start to build your confidence is to reflect on your accomplishments.

When emotional situations happen, this will assure you that you can handle anything.

- **Competence:** When you have the ability to complete tasks with quality based on specific timelines, your competence levels are high. Your competency involves learned skills combined with a bit of rational thinking and a consideration of the negative impact of what you are not supposed to do. This will enable you to handle emotional situations with careful analysis and actions that will lead to outcomes that ensure your well-being.

- **Connections:** These play a wide variety of roles in building your resilience when you are faced with emotionally provoking situations. Connections encourage you to stop and consider who will be negatively impacted if you give in to a highly emotional urge. Additionally, the support from your friends is great at keeping you focused in a positive way, knowing that you will receive all the help you need if things get worse.

- **Character:** Your character is based on a moral compass that prevents you from doing or saying certain things, even when no one you know is watching. For example, if it is out of your character for you to engage in alcohol and drug usage, then you will not do it when an intense emotional situation happens.

- **Contribution:** By figuring out how you can contribute to the improvement of the world and making an effort to work in that direction, you will have a sense of fulfillment that will make you easily persevere during emotional situations. This is why volunteering during your teenage years is very important.

- **Coping:** Using emotional coping strategies such as meditation, exercise, and mindfulness will build your emotional resilience as well.
- **Control:** There is nothing wrong with being emotional when things do not go according to our plans or when someone intentionally does something to us; however, having self-control is very important regardless of your age.

The Role of Emotional Intelligence

Emotional intelligence is the ability to recognize, process, show, manage, measure, and use emotions in a way that enables you to connect and relate well with other people. With emotional intelligence, you will be able to navigate through the emotional dramas that come from social media, friendships, romantic relationships, school stress, first-time employment, and much more. There are four components to emotional intelligence that you should be aware of:

- **Perceiving emotions:** There are times when we are heavily reliant on using verbal communication to know how people feel, but emotional intelligence will enable you to pick up an idea of how someone feels from their behavior, facial expressions, and body language, even if they do not verbally tell you how they are feeling.

- **Reasoning with emotions:** Emotional intelligence allows you to have a logical understanding of why a particular emotion is being experienced. Without this skill, it might be impossible to recognize and accept how someone is feeling.
- **Understanding emotions:** This means knowing how emotions operate and how to increase or decrease them. For example, with emotional intelligence, you would know how to calm down an angry or hyperactive younger sibling to make them stop playing with a dangerous object.
- **Management of emotions:** This is the ability to regulate your emotions and express them effectively, even when still being impacted by what stimulated the emotion. For example, if a person slams a door in your face without warning, you would expect them to apologize or at least explain their anger. If they continue by laughing in your face and daring you to fight back, it is important to know how to avoid sinking to their level and making the situation worse. You can manage your responsive anger with a sense of reasoning that allows you to assertively stand up for yourself without becoming aggressive.

How EI Builds Emotional Resilience

It is rare to be emotionally intelligent but not emotionally resilient because one naturally nourishes the other through the following pathways:

- **Self-awareness:** Emotional intelligence involves having self-awareness; this means that you will be able to look at an emotion you are feeling from a different point of view and figure out ways to manage yourself effectively.
- **Social adaptivity:** Emotional intelligence enables you to handle emotional changes effectively. This is important if you have a super active social media presence that is connected to your real life at school.
- **Empathy:** The ability to understand how others are feeling when they behave negatively towards us will enable us to have more control of our feelings and react in a constructive, communicative manner.

CBT PRINCIPLES FOR ENHANCING RESILIENCE

Cognitive Flexibility

Cognitive flexibility allows you to change your thought patterns to align them with reality and your core values and be able to take the necessary actions that lead to the outcomes you desire. For example, if you've always had concerns about the things that could be lurking in the darkness, and suddenly, a power outage happens when you are alone at home, cognitive flexibility enables you to reason that there has never been any evidence of strange creatures in the dark. You can acknowledge the fact that it may be hard for you to see, but instead of giving in to panic, this CBT principle allows you to focus on practical solutions and either comfort yourself with the flashlight on your phone or challenge your fears further by going to a safe place outside. Embracing cognitive flexibility has empowered a lot of people to remain emotionally stable.

Challenging Limiting Beliefs

Limiting beliefs are conditions you set on yourself not to do or engage in certain activities because of some perceived limitations that you believe you have. Some common limiting beliefs that teenagers have, and their leading consequences, are as follows:

- Thinking you are too young to be heartbroken may prevent you from processing disappointment in romantic relationships. This may lead you into negative behavioral tendencies that you may not recognize as a result of your unresolved emotions.
- Restrictive gender- and sexuality-based beliefs may be more pronounced during your teenage years due to peer pressure, the imposed beliefs of caregivers, and many other influential sources of social norms.
- Believing that they are not good at a particular subject causes many teenagers to make no effort to improve academically; then, when test dates are near, they get stressed out and worried about their overall academic performance, and this can push people into mental health crises.
- The assumption that you are predestined for failure is a very big deal during our teenage years. This belief is not only associated with academics but also with all general areas of life such as relationships and the ability to be

independent. If you hold this belief, the moment that you fail at one thing, you'll likely have a surge of emotions that lead to drastically negative thoughts and dramatic assumptions about how you will never succeed at anything in life.

The best way to challenge limiting beliefs is to evaluate the way you think. Follow the process below:

1. **Write down your limiting beliefs:** Writing things down creates a sense that you are confining them to a piece of paper which allows you to take a much different perspective. It also allows you to keep track of these beliefs.
2. **Clarify the belief:** Examine the belief, and try to identify any valid reasons for holding the belief. For example, if you believe that you are too short to try out for the school basketball team, you can clarify that height is not actually a nonnegotiable requirement to play basketball.
3. **Evidence for the belief:** Continuing with the example of height and playing basketball, you can check if there is a rule that restricts people of a certain height or lower from playing basketball for school teams in your region.
4. **Alternative points of view:** Okay, maybe you find out that there is no rule that restricts short people from playing basketball, but you may be discouraged to find that statistics show that many basketball players are tall. However, people as short as 5' 3" have played in the NBA, so you can challenge your belief with a different

point of view that recognizes other physical capabilities, like speed.

5. **Implications and consequences:** Identify the consequences costs of having such a belief; for example, believing that you can't play basketball because your height is lower than most standard players will make you have low self-esteem when you are around tall people and hold you back from something where you could be really successful. However, trying out for the basketball team will boost your confidence with the knowledge that you have the courage to take risks and learn new skills.

How Bill Turned Failure into Success

Bill had never learned how to ride a bike. At 15, he was so afraid of falling off a bicycle that he would always change the topic whenever his friends tried to bring it up. He believed that falling off a bike would cause him to break his bones and send him to the ICU. But when school was out for the holidays, his cousin—who is about the same age as him—came from out of town for a visit. During the visit, he saw his cousin fall off a bike. Bill rushed to him, scared and expecting the worst, but his cousin got up, picked up his bike, and started riding it again. In that moment, Bill realized how incorrect his belief had been; he had always known that people fall off their bikes and usually get back up without any injuries, but seeing it in person really drove home how irrational his fear had become. With the help of his cousin, Bill started practicing how to ride a bike, mainly because he wanted to change his belief that falling off a bike would result in being sent to the ICU. He fell a few times, laughed, and each time, he got back up. Soon, the entire experience with the bike turned into an activity of learning how to fall off safely without getting hurt. Once the holiday break from school ended, Bill enrolled in a program for stunt bikers.

PRACTICAL EXERCISES TO BUILD RESILIENCE

There are many exercises and practices that you can implement to build your resilience even further.

Daily Journaling Practices

As mentioned earlier, writing down your thoughts and feelings enables you to look at your feelings from different perspectives that can guide you through the process. The benefits of journaling are as follows:

- **Reduction of stress and emotional buildup:** By writing these thoughts and feelings down on paper, this process acts as an outlet.
- **Improved cognition:** The creative process of writing can lead to the ability to challenge your unhealthy beliefs in the moment and enable you to handle emotional changes effectively.
- **Improved ability to be present with your current emotions:** Journaling has a component of mindfulness. This will prevent emotional overload from memories of past experiences and fears of the future.

It can be extremely helpful to schedule a regular time to practice journaling. This will ensure that you are the most prepared to journal during the times when you are emotional.

Mindfulness and Grounding Techniques

Practicing mindfulness such as breathing techniques or the 5-4-3-2-1 grounding exercise can build your resilience because you will start becoming more present and dealing with the emotions at hand, preventing any emotions from your past experiences or fears of the future from disrupting your present situation. You can utilize mindfulness techniques to cope with many common teenage stressors like the fear of failing a test or the worry of not finding the right person to date.

Building a Support Structure

It's important to try to make connections with people who have the emotional and mental capacity to understand you when you're dealing with an intense emotional situation. It's not easy to tell if you have the right people in your circles for support, but watching how some of your friends treat other people in bad situations can indicate whether they are capable of the level of empathy you deserve. This will give you an idea of what to expect when you start going through a rough situation, and knowing that they will support you in building your resilience can itself help you to feel some emotional relief and strength.

How Sarah's Support Community Helped Her

Sarah is a 19-year-old girl who lost her chance of going to college when she got close to the lowest possible score in her SATs. This situation was made worse by her boyfriend breaking up with her. Disappointed in herself for failing to get into college and feeling blindsided and betrayed by her now ex-boyfriend, Sarah became convinced that she was not good enough for anything. The story of her situation spread throughout her neighborhood, including to the seniors living in the retirement home where Sarah volunteered to read for them. When they heard the story of what happened to Sarah, they reached out to her and comforted her with kind words about her personality. They told her how nice she was and how lucky the community was to have her around. Sarah's thoughts of not being good enough and her belief in her uselessness faded away. Then, one of the seniors at the retirement home arranged for her to take the SATs again in two months. Other people in the retirement home offered her their support through tutoring. Two months and ten days later Sarah found out that she passed the tests with a good score and was later accepted into the same college where she was rejected the previous semester.

Inspiring Positive Energy

"Your state of mind and attitude will undoubtedly affect other people. When you can look on the bright side of life, you will inspire others to do the same."

STEVE JEFFERSON AND DAVE MORROW

Wouldn't it be great if they taught CBT skills in school? You might be thinking how much easier your life might have been if you'd known these strategies sooner.

But here's the thing: You know them now, and they're not reserved only for your teenage years – they're something you'll always have, and you'll be able to fall back on them time and time again.

In fact, I believe they're something we should all know about. The energy we put out into the world makes a difference in what we see coming back to us. That's because when we're feeling confident and happy, those around us feel at ease, and they give us positive energy back; when we're anxious or angry, they may feel guarded, and we're probably not going to feel the positive energy that would make us feel more at ease. It's a cycle, and if everyone was aware of what they could do to handle their own stress, not only would more people be happier, but they'd encounter more joy around them too.

With this in mind, I'd like to ask for your help in spreading awareness – and the great news is, that it will only take a few minutes of your time.

By leaving a review of this book on Amazon, you'll help other people like you to access these skills and begin their own journey to conquer the chaos.

Every review acts as a roadmap, guiding new readers to find the information they're looking for: Your review makes more difference than you realize.

Thank you so much for your support. You're making an amazing contribution.

Scan the QR code below to leave your review.

CHAPTER 7

STEPPING INTO ADULTHOOD —FUTURE FEARS AND HOW TO OVERCOME THEM

When growing up, we always admire the freedoms and possibilities that come with adulthood. It always seems like adults have a life without consequences—no one telling them what to do; having more money and freedom to buy all the clothes, snacks, toys, and treats that they want. This rose-tinted belief paints a bright future and shapes our dreams according to often-unrealistic ideals, but SMART goals provide real, tangible structure to our journey into adulthood. Using a technique such as this as a framework for your intentions ensures that you exercise realism by assessing the conditions of your circumstances.

For most of us, our teen years challenge our childhood ideas of adulthood as we are met with barriers like high academic performance criteria and circumstances shaped by financial conditions; personal skills, strengths, and weaknesses; unrealistic romantic endings; and irrational beauty standards. This has led many people to experience stress when thinking about the prospect of adulthood. What's important to remember, however, is that while many aspects of your opportunities are outside of your control, you are still the ultimate master of your own destiny; and you can only get out of life what you put in, so it's essential to learn how to overcome your anxieties about adulthood. Thankfully, CBT holds the answers here too!

THE TRANSITION TO ADULTHOOD

Experts have discovered that the teenage transition to adulthood is marked by several characteristics. The first and most important is that the years that mark your entrance into adulthood—between 18 and 25—have been recognized as practically and emotionally separate from adolescence and adulthood; this means that when you are 18 or 19, you will no longer feel like a teenager, but you'll likely still lack the confidence or skills to function independently as an adult. This can lead to emotional health issues, a loss of a sense of belonging or identity, and a fear of being unable to keep up with newfound responsibilities. For some people, this feels even harder than being a teenager; for others, it marks the beginning of a period of growth toward inner peace; and the biggest determining factor in how you experience this transition is often how prepared you feel to face it.

This transition is not marked by turning a year older on your birthday; it is marked by how society begins to treat you. You will be expected to be independent in almost all areas of your life, leading to a high reduction in emotional, mental, and financial support. The stressors of teenage life are often enough to trigger anxiety, so if you have not emotionally processed these upcoming changes, adding on the pressures of this transitional period can increase the feelings and thoughts that can make your life seem chaotic. Breaking down some of the most common sources of anxiety during this time can help to challenge negative thoughts about becoming an adult.

Common Fears That Teens Face

Whether you have reached 18 or not, it is important to know the types of fears that you might experience when coming close to adulthood:

- **Career choices:** In addition to needing to choose a career path that suits you, our rapidly changing world can be a source of professional anxiety. The uncertainty of what the future looks like for many careers can leave you wondering whether the career you want to dedicate your life to is going to be relevant in the long term. Parents and other mentors might tell you to have multiple career options open to secure your future, but this just adds to the workload of preparing for adulthood. You may also be faced with fears of choosing the wrong career or letting your family down if things don't work out. Another challenge you may face is wondering if you will even like the careers that will allow you to earn enough money for the quality of life that you want.

- **Financial independence:** Many teenagers approaching adulthood are faced with the expectation to move out of their parents' or guardians' homes. This means being able to pay rent. However, it is very hard to see how that will be possible if you completely focus on your studies in college. This generates a lot of anxiety. Likewise, the realization of other financial responsibilities like groceries, electricity, WiFi, and even the need to visit your friends back at home can make you feel worried about your financial future.
- **Social changes:** Teenagers approaching adulthood are often afraid of loneliness and the loss of a strong support system that came from high school friends, each of whom are moving on to their own adult commitments. Those in romantic relationships will often experience intense fears of heartbreak due to the number of changes that can lead to severe self-esteem issues during this period.

Failure to Launch

Failure to launch is a situation where a person continues to depend on their parents or guardians for their needs such as shelter and food well into adulthood. This can be due to a debilitating fear of facing the challenges of this transitional period head-on. Extreme societal expectations can lead to young adults finding it difficult to take the step. Alcohol and drug abuse can also be an issue when a young adult can't properly manage their behavior or make rational decisions, even if they have a job that gives them enough income to pay the rent on their own apartment. However, it's important to remember that a person who has had a "failure to launch" has usually actually been failed by the people and systems that were supposed to help them prepare for adulthood, so it's not something to be ashamed of. Learning techniques that help manage anxieties about the future can help to both prevent and treat a failure to launch.

UNPACKING FUTURE ANXIETIES

You are likely going to face some future anxiety in at least one area of your life when approaching adulthood, and overcoming these challenges is a key step in creating the foundation of the confidence and self-esteem that you will take into your adult years. This section will help you understand how future anxieties are shaped in order to make the application of CBT tools and techniques effective.

Origins of Future Fears

Fears of the future originate from the following main categories:

- **Past experiences:** Past experiences like failures, embarrassing moments, or situations that caused you to make harsh judgments about yourself can lead you to believe that your future will be shaped by the same experiences. People use past experiences to predict their futures because of a conditioning of familiarity. This makes us expect to continue having the same levels of social connection, to keep living in the same type of house, and to stay going to the same schools; if any or all of these circumstances are not desirable, then we will experience fear of the future.

- **Societal expectations:** There are many expectations that young adults are led to believe they should live up to. For example, young adults are often expected to make as many romantic connections as possible to have a better chance of finding a suitable partner to settle down with. However, such expectations generate a lot of insecurity as they usually come with beauty standards that do not capture the diversity of the beauty of different teenagers. More specifically, girls often fear that they may not be able to develop the body types that reflect the beauty standards of popular culture. This makes them experience low self-esteem and have future fears of loneliness. For boys, the need to project a "player" persona can cause them to disrespect their own boundaries of consent.

- **The need to fit in:** Fitting in is a very important concept because this is how teenagers make connections and have interactions that define their identity in a group setting. However, this may cause intense fears of the future for teenagers who don't think or feel that their values or principles will make them fit in. For example, a teenager who knows that their plans for the future will require them to move to a new city where their personal opinions on politics and religion will go against the grain may find themself wishing that they could conform and be like many of the people living in that city. This will lead to a crisis of identity in which they will feel torn between fitting in with the people of a different city and remaining true to the beliefs of their friends and family when they visit home in the future.

The Paralysis of Overthinking

When overthinking reaches a critical stage, it becomes *rumination*—a cycle of negative thoughts that devolves to the point that a person becomes so absorbed in the related emotions that they become a normal part of their daily life. It is difficult to know when overthinking has become so serious that it threatens your overall well-being. Concerns about the future have been identified as one of the leading reasons for rumination. Rumination will paralyze your rational decision-making in the present and can lead to impulsive, reckless behavior or the development of a mental illness. For example, a person who ruminates on whether they will fit in when they move to another city for college may develop a social anxiety disorder that impacts them even with people they know and used to feel safe with.

CBT TECHNIQUES TO COMBAT FUTURE ANXIETIES

With the use of CBT techniques and tools, you can overcome any fears of approaching adulthood and continue to be effective as a teenager. Use the following techniques to combat future anxieties.

Techniques to Reduce Worry

Worries are the thoughts that are prompted by or that prompt feelings such as fear. Therefore, by reducing the frequency or severity of your worries, you will be able to easily cope with other emotions. Additionally, with low levels of worry, you will always trust that things will turn out okay. The proven CBT techniques for reducing worry are as follows:

- **Identifying and clarifying the feared outcomes:** Once you have identified how things could turn out badly, you must remember that possible outcomes are made-up scenarios— not a guarantee of reality. This will enable you to consider that you might be wrong. However, whether you end up being wrong or right, it is important to check whether your dreaded future could even possibly happen. For example, if you fear that you will not get accepted into a particular college because you didn't do well on your final exams, then you can check the minimum academic requirement to get accepted. After checking, you might be surprised that the scores needed are much lower than you feared. Your worrying can also come from one of the sources described in the previous section.
- **Using Socratic questioning:** It's possible that your worries are associated with certain limiting beliefs about your past experiences—like how you previously failed a test at school and worry that the final exams will result in the same outcome because you don't believe that you have the capacity to get good grades.

Use the Socratic thinking strategies explained in the last chapter to overcome limiting beliefs.

- **Explore coping strategies for the feared outcome:** In the event of a true catastrophe, where simply put, it would take a miracle for things to work out in your favor, it helps to be prepared by having considered how you would adjust to the situation. For example, if you worry that failing the exams and not getting accepted into college is a true possibility, you may come up with a back-up plan to repeat the grade next year and study hard to prepare for the exams. Knowing that you have a plan, if worse comes to worst, allows you to step back from your worries and focus on what's within your control in the here and now.

- **Using exposure methods:** Exposing yourself to similar feared outcomes would greatly reduce your anxiety. For example, worries about not getting accepted into college based on fears of failing your final exams can be addressed by taking practice exams and using the scores to identify areas of focus for further study. If for any particular reason, your scores in one practice test end up being higher than you thought, then you will find your anxieties greatly reduced, allowing you to take the final exam without worrying.

- **Welcoming uncertainty:** Uncertainty makes everyone uncomfortable but you can greatly reduce the associated worries it might bring by becoming comfortable with uncertainty. You can achieve this with practice, like trying out for a sports team, trusting that a crush will return a DM, or attempting to make people in your class laugh. These small activities might make you feel overly cautious, but as you continue practicing, you will reduce your worries.

- **Writing down the worry in detail:** This process is called *in vivo therapy* in one of the many CBT techniques, meaning imaginary exposure to your worry. By writing your future worries down and reading them out aloud, you will have some room to process the information from another perspective, like asking yourself if you have gathered enough evidence to accurately predict that things will indeed turn out that way.

- **Structure your worry time:** Anxiety works like waves of water, it begins, then rises, and finally, falls; so, when you recognize the pattern and develop a way to stimulate and release the worry, it is best to arrange a time when you will induce and experience the worry until it subsides. This will prevent the worries from sneaking up on you at a time when you really need to be using your mind and emotions toward constructive activities.

Staying Present

This involves the practice of mindfulness, by doing exercises like the 5-4-3-2-1 technique or deep breathing and focusing on the present, recognizing that your future has multiple possibilities that might surprise you. Meditate on how you feared the worst about a particular situation yet when it happened, you found that things turned out ok and you thought about how silly it was that it worried you so much.

Five Visualization Exercises to Calm the Mind

These meditation exercises are best suited for worries that make you not want to complete your immediate tasks like studying or doing your homework:

- **Color breathing:** This involves assigning colors to emotions that you want to feel and then focusing on that color while you take deep breaths.
- **Compassion meditation:** This is a type of meditation that involves building kind and loving thoughts and emotions about yourself. Through very slow breaths, you can create a sense of emotional safety and use self-compassion to confront future worries of failure.
- **Progressive muscle relaxation:** When future anxieties build up, your body may enter a fight-or-flight response as if a perceived threatening future outcome is happening in real-time. Then, your muscles may become tense. Counterintuitively, you can relax them by purposely tensing one muscle group at a time for 30–60 seconds before releasing.
- **Guided imagery:** This form of meditation involves the visualization of places, people, or things that make you feel calm and happy. For example, focusing on your favorite ice cream flavor and all the toppings on a hot day can make you feel relaxed.

- **Goal visualization:** Future fears of failure can be addressed by this exercise. It involves imagining yourself having accomplished your goals and feeling the emotions that come with the achievements.

How Jacob Passed His Agricultural Science Exam

Jacob was 16 when he realized that he'd never believed he could fully understand agricultural science because he grew up in the city and had never visited a farm. He had paid little attention to the subject and sometimes even skipped the lessons. Since he was always an exceptional student in other subjects like physics, chemistry, and biology, the school administration did not make much of an issue with his lack of interest. When the final exams started drawing near, Jacob wanted to pass the agricultural science test as he always did with his other subjects. His core values came through because he didn't consider himself a quitter, so he decided to do the best he could with the prep time he had left. To his amazement, he found that his biology knowledge gave him a foundational basis for the subject, and that boosted his confidence to try to understand the rest of the syllabus. He passed the test with a very high score, and to this day, as a college graduate, he tells the story of how he would have missed out on another achievement if he had given in to his fears.

CHAPTER 8
CULTIVATING SELF CONFIDENCE—MIRROR TALKS AND BEYOND

One of the true powers of confidence is the ability to make your own choices; it's about the power to know that the judgments of others are usually based on their own insecurities and to prioritize your own opinion, comfort, and values. Confidence is not something that appears automatically; it requires a process of learning and adjusting certain beliefs about yourself. As a result of the number of stressors and unfair expectations placed upon teenagers that we have discussed up to this point, it can be difficult for most young people to build confidence. Sadly, materialistic societal norms have caused a lot of teenagers to equate confidence with wealth-based ego and things like luxury cars or expensive clothes.

THE IMPORTANCE OF SELF-CONFIDENCE

Self-confidence is the strong belief that our own natural abilities and characteristics are good enough to get us through any situation and acquire what we need. Confidence is often associated with self-worth or self-value and an ability to be assertive.

Understanding Self-Worth

Having self-worth involves feeling secure in one's sense of self without the need for validation. There are a lot of benefits that come from self-worth:

- **Meeting your needs:** Believing in your own worth fosters a greater commitment to achieving goals that fulfill your needs because you believe you deserve it. Your own confidence in your worth and the validity of your needs also encourages that same belief in other people, who will try their best to treat you with the same respect with which you treat yourself.
- **Solving problems confidently:** Your self-worth will push you to solve problems because you believe you deserve to live a life without constant stress; additionally, because self-worth involves recognizing your own abilities, you will approach problems with the confidence to solve them.
- **Being more decisive:** Having self-worth will make your decision-making process easier and more direct because you'll understand and respect your own core values, boundaries, and limitations with ease.

- **Maintaining healthier relationships:** You will be able to treat people in the same manner that you would want to be treated based on your self-worth, helping you to develop and maintain stronger, more supportive connections.

For all of these reasons and more, self-worth has been known to have a positive effect on people's mental health. For example, fears of ending up with a bad career or making mistakes can be greatly avoided when you believe in your own worth outside of external measures of success, and this greatly minimizes the possibility of depressing thoughts and other related anxieties.

Why Confidence Matters

One of the key reasons why confidence is so crucial is that it allows you to become comfortable with the idea of having problems. This means that anxieties that come from the fear of problems or uncertainties will be greatly reduced or even eliminated. Many people will tell you how difficult adulthood is or how stressful college life can be, and though you can listen respectfully it's vital to reflect on the confidence you have rather than be carried away with negative emotions.

Additionally, your confidence will also prevent you from making strong judgments about people who discouragingly tell you things are very hard or impossible to do; your positive response while recognizing their perspectives of things will set new norms of compassion and empathy. This can even make these discouragers curious about your natural abilities and talent, which can help them reframe their own thoughts and lead to great relationships.

MIRROR TALKS—A JOURNEY INWARDS

In the introduction to this chapter, it was emphasized that confidence is not based on material possessions or what people are saying about you; placing value or hinging your own worth on these things can actually be a result of low confidence rather than what confidence really is. Through an idea called *mirror talks,* you can learn to focus inward and build true confidence.

A mirror talk, as the name implies, is the exercise of looking at yourself in the mirror and engaging in positive self-talk that brings self-recognition of your natural abilities and characteristics. Your mirror—which you may have mostly been using to criticize your own appearances up until now—can make this process feel uncomfortable. However, mirror talks have been proven to be a very powerful self-confidence-building innovation. This technique was initially developed by Louise Hay, a transformational teacher who has authored two books titled *Mirror Works: 21 Days to Heal Your Life* and *Heal Your Body.* The simplest approach to practicing mirror talks is as follows:

1. Stand or sit in front of a mirror and look at your reflection. Try to relax as much as possible and say that you love yourself, that you have accepted yourself, and that you are safe. Do this for five minutes, once a day during the first week.

2. Increase the time you spend looking in the mirror and repeating the words of self-love, self-acceptance, and safety. Invest up to 10 minutes per session twice per day in the second week.

These steps seem fairly easy for anyone to do but to make this technique as impactful as possible, it is recommended that you follow the listed guidelines on how to do the exercises effectively:

- **Exercise space conditions:** Make sure that the space you will use to practice mirror talks feels safe and enables you to relax. Trying to force yourself to relax will not make the words resonate with the energy inside yourself when you say them.
- **Use affirmations that go beyond physical appearances:** Physical appearances can be deceiving because the lenses that we use to define physical beauty are limited. Use words that are based on your inner qualities like being compassionate, creative, and wonderful.
- **Make it a daily practice:** Once you make mirror talks a daily practice, you will find it easy to do the exercise in different environments and for different confidence-building challenges, from developing academic confidence to affirming your own abilities for auditioning for a national talent show.

Confidence is based on believing in yourself, and looking at yourself in the mirror while saying positive, affirmational phrases can help you find that belief.

Benefits of Regular Mirror Talks

Think about building confidence with mirror talks in the same manner as muscles responding to exercise by staying in shape; mirror talks should be embraced as a lifestyle to have the following benefits:

- **Reinforcing self-belief:** With every single day that you engage in a mirror talk, your self-belief becomes more fixed in your mind, as do the possibilities for maximizing it. With this mindset, challenges will never feel like an ambush, meaning that you will never feel like retreating or giving up.
- **Overcoming negative self-talk:** Negative self-talk always finds its way in at the first chance when something goes wrong, but confidence is your mind's immune system, fighting off these harmful intrusions. With the self-worth built during mirror-talking sessions, you will not be too hard on yourself, even in situations where you know you've made avoidable mistakes. Instead, you will take responsibility for the mistake and work towards fixing the issue.
- **Strengthening self-acceptance:** Self-acceptance challenges are common, regardless of a person's age. Strengthening self-acceptance during your teenage years will minimize the fears associated with applying

for college or getting involved in a romantic relationship.

- **Increasing mindfulness and self-awareness:** Wording your mirror-talk affirmations in the present tense minimizes the negative impact of past mistakes and future fears of failure on your confidence.
- **Boosting your mood and emotional well-being:** When you engage in positive self-talk several times each day, you will likely stay in a positive mood while maximizing the benefits that come from being in a good mood as well.

BEYOND MIRROR TALK—BUILDING A CONFIDENT SELF

Since we now know that confidence is very different from arrogance, we can understand that there is no such thing as too much confidence when it comes to pursuing or engaging in many of life's possibilities, opportunities, and challenges. This section will introduce confidence-building methods that have been proven effective in the lives of many other people.

Adopting a Growth Mindset

A growth mindset is a way of thinking that challenges the idea that skills and talents are fixed and moves a person towards recognizing that both the least and most talented people in the world continue growing through new experiences, learning, and hard work. In the context of self-confidence, a growth mindset will always make you explore ways to continue developing your natural skills and talents.

With a fixed mindset, on the other hand, many talented and skillful individuals who experience failure or make a silly mistake can go on a downward spiral and lose touch with their confidence. A growth mindset will encourage you to look at failures and mistakes as part of the process of growing, enabling you to be highly resilient against emotional setbacks.

Overcoming a fixed mindset is not always easy, but one of the ways that you can do so is by getting rid of limiting beliefs. This also involves reducing dependence on the praise and admiration you receive from other people—some exceptionally gifted people have always received this praise and thus have never learned to validate themselves, becoming dependent on external commendations to maintain their self-esteem, leaving them with no self-confidence. Of course, you should enjoy praise when you receive it, but by developing a growth mindset, you will keep an open mind to the possibilities of growth and build resilience against the negative impacts of failure.

Creating a Positive Affirmation Routine

Positive affirmations are praises that we say to ourselves for things that we have achieved and for the way we are. While these are most effectively used as part of a mirror-talk routine, they can also become your mental mantras or go-to pep talks in times of distress. It can be very difficult to ignore the increasingly loud inner critic of your mind when you make a mistake or fail at something, especially when your brain has been trained to think negative thoughts even at the best of times. Thankfully, however, experts have shown that people can use the purposeful repetition of positive messages to "rewrite" these brain superhighways and replace them with positive self-images to stimulate positive emotions. Therefore, by using affirmations, you will be able to be confident all the time.

In addition to using affirmations that build your confidence and address your circumstances, it's important to use relevant, positive affirmations that are suited to the common challenges of being a teenager, even if you don't currently find yourself directly facing those challenges. This will improve your emotional and mental capacity to deal with these issues effectively if they arise.

Just like many of the other exercises in this book, affirmations should become a part of your life. There are three easy steps that every teenager can take when starting their practice of affirmations:

1. Pick your affirmation: This involves three considerations—what you want to use the affirmation for, keeping the affirmation short enough to make it easy to say, and making sure that it is authentic. For example, you can pick an affirmation that says "I am excellent" for the purpose of passing a test and to build an understanding that excellence is something that we all have whether we pass or fail tests.

2. Know when to use it: Use the affirmation to challenge negative thoughts and build positive mental patterns around negativity triggers. Continuing with the example in the first step, you could use the affirmation before you study to give you the motivation to learn and to build positive, calm patterns in academic environments.

3. Keep using it: When you keep using an affirmation even after the completion of its initial purpose, this strengthens your belief in the authenticity of the affirmation and reinforces the positive mental pathways further.

Now that you have an understanding of the power of affirmations, take the action of writing them down and saying them.

CHAPTER 9
PRACTICAL STEPS TO INTEGRATE CBT INTO TEEN LIFE

How nice would it be to see every challenge as a stepping stone rather than a permanent barrier to what you want? To turn setbacks into setups that will push you even further than you thought you would ever reach? By making CBT techniques a part of your everyday life, you will be able to achieve the following:

- build and grow your resilience
- shift your perspectives to more beneficial ones
- implement an effective goal-reaching process
- adapt well to changes
- learn how to identify and manage the emotions of others to make effective connections
- experience feelings of success while on the journey to specific goals
- establish enough forward momentum in life to be consistent and excel

- acknowledge and enjoy small victories
- develop innovative thinking

This book has been consistent in its emphasis on the key steps to create a life you want through the effective management of your thoughts, feelings, and behaviors. It is important that you not only see CBT techniques as a means to an end but recognize it as a lifestyle that maintains your emotional and mental well-being.

ESTABLISHING A DAILY REFLECTION ROUTINE

A daily reflection routine involves doing a set of activities every day in the same sequence. Whenever people carry out a routine, they build confidence, safe in the knowledge that their expectations for the benefits of performing the routine will be met.

Why Reflection Matters

You will find that a lot of successful people talk about and encourage others to practice reflection. Self-reflection is the practice of looking at your feelings, thoughts, and behaviors from a broad perspective. The general approach is to focus on the *what* rather than the *why* of thinking, feeling, or acting the way that you do. Self-reflection is a bridge toward self-awareness because it makes you focus on what and how things really are, not what you want them to be. It also helps you to make sense of your personal identity through the process of identifying your unique qualities. By looking at yourself objectively, you will be able to change your thoughts, behaviors, and feelings in accordance with what your present circumstances demand to ensure your overall well-being.

Introspection

Introspection is a deeper, more specific part of self-reflection that involves analyzing your thoughts and emotions to understand or indirectly change them. Introspection, unlike general reflection, does not focus on the present moment; nor does it focus on change. Instead, introspection illuminates the patterns and processes of your mental and emotional landscape. For example, you can be introspective about your past feelings and thoughts, enabling you to recognize how particular conditions in your environment can trigger those emotional patterns. However, introspection does not involve placing blame on those conditions; rather, it empowers you to acknowledge what was within your control, take responsibility for your reactions to difficult circumstances, and understand how to respond effectively in the future. By taking responsibility for what you *can* change—your own inner world—you remove the power that difficult conditions once held over you and place it in your hands (or head); this is a key step towards healing, growth, and the ability to manage your emotions. Introspection has been shown to be very powerful in overcoming addiction, breaking patterns of repeated mistakes, and building self-worth.

Starting Simple

Self-reflection exercises can be adapted to suit your personal needs and goals. However, it is important to start with the basic setup:

1. **Choose an area of life to reflect on:** There are obviously lots of things going on in each area of your life; when you engage in self-reflection, it's important to focus on the most important things to get the most bang for your introspective buck. For example, if you have a rich online life, you can choose to reflect on how you handle social media posts from your friends recognizing the emotions and thoughts you have about that area of your life and how they influence your behavior.

2. **Write down each reflection exercise in a journal:** It is a good idea to write down the topics you reflect on and your discoveries about the thoughts, feelings, and behaviors that you identified during the exercise. This both helps you gain perspective and allows you to track your emotional growth.

3. **Find a pattern:** Reflect on how you have been acting in the past year, six months, or any chosen amount of time. Identify the emotions and thoughts that prompted, or were prompted by, those actions. Then, develop a plan to change the negative patterns of those emotions and feelings by using the CBT techniques to overcome the negative actions.

4. **Set a goal:** The notes in your journal and the pattern you have identified can be used as a basis to set your CBT goals, such as using thought reframing to reduce how often you feel sad when you see your friends make wonderful social media posts. Don't forget to make sure that your goal is set by SMART standards.

5. **Make adjustments:** You may need to make adjustments to your self-reflection routine as you grow and develop more self-awareness. You may start out by reading your self-reflection journal notes to aid your process, but with time, you might be able to jump straight to addressing feelings that you want to work on.

6. **Evaluate the changes made:** Did you see an improvement in the way that you thought, acted, and behaved after becoming more self-aware?

7. **Repeat:** Repeat these basic steps for one area of your life you want to reflect on as many times as necessary. Then, use the same steps when moving on to another area.

You can continue to use these steps repeatedly for years, and the exercise will still be effective.

Gratitude Journals

Gratitude journaling has a similar but more positive effect to reflection. It involves the exercise of writing, typing, or recording things that you are grateful for. This is most effective when practiced for 15 minutes at least three days a week. You start in the same way as you do with introspection—by going over a time when you can recognize moments that you are grateful for. It is important to be specific and avoid generalizations such as being grateful for the sun that shined so magnificently; even though the recognition of such general things is also important, your gratitude journal has to be deeply connected to you and your experiences, so you could instead write about being grateful for the way the rays of the sun made your skin feel pleasantly warm or your gratitude for when a friend came over for a visit.

While documenting your lists of things that you are grateful for, it can also be helpful to reflect on how difficult things would have been in that situation without the listed things. Remember, it doesn't matter how big or small the things that you are grateful for are; what's most important is to reflect on the positive experience of them. For example, your teacher commending you for putting in good effort with your homework assignments may have made you swell with pride and reminded you that you are capable of reaching your goals; being specific in this way will prevent you from taking things for granted.

How Ashley Used Journal Prompts to Find That Her Life Was Not That Bad

Ashley is a 15-year-old girl who lives with her loving single mother, Deirdre, who dedicates much of her time to Ashley's well-being. But for a long time, Deirdre talked about how things were not done according to her standards or expectations; Ashley's life felt miserable. Then, one day, her school counselor introduced her to journal prompts—lists of questions that helped her find a way of being grateful for the life she had, having pride in who she was, and learning lessons about how she could have done things differently. Ashley got angry at her mother for making her feel that she was ungrateful and went to lock herself in her room, but the self-awareness she had gained through journaling also helped her to recognize that she had overreacted, and she continued writing about her emotions until she felt ready to assertively communicate that she deserved more credit and respect. After extending empathy to herself, Ashley realized that she could also be compassionate to her stressed-out mother while still setting healthy boundaries. With some open communication, both Ashley and Deirdre were able to process their emotions, and though, from the outside, it didn't look as though the daily actions of their lives had changed much, they were much more content. Ashley was surprised that she found the entire experience emotionally and mentally uplifting.

INTEGRATING COGNITIVE RESTRUCTURING

With effective cognitive restructuring, the process of managing your thoughts and emotions can be done in a very fast way; this is important because we live in a world that is moving at a very fast pace.

Catch It, Check It, Change It

This three-step activity is specifically designed for teenagers and is meant to prevent or break a negative cycle of emotions and thoughts that lead to anxiety or depression:

1. **Catch it**: Whenever you feel sad, worried, angry, or experience any other kind of negative emotion, catch your thoughts and find any that are responsible for the emotion. For example, you may be feeling sad all of a sudden, but with some self-reflection, you could find that you've been having passing thoughts that a friend doesn't care about you because they haven't replied to your text.

2. **Check it**: This step is about verifying the thought responsible for the negative feeling. Continuing with the example in the first step, you may want to check if your friend has indeed received your text or if an absence of their usual Snapchat story posts points to them being away from their phone. If they are clearly actively online, the feeling of sadness may be intensified, making the next step important.

3. **Change it**: This final step involves addressing the thought with other perspectives that will replace it. Continuing with the example above, you can challenge the thought with considerations that maybe your friend is at a family event where taking photos is okay but having a text conversation would come across as rude. You might also consider that they could be having a difficult day, posting online to distract themselves and

receive validation but feeling unable to focus on chatting. All of these considerations will change the thought, and the feeling will reduce accordingly.

Practical Scenarios

CBT restructuring can come in handy in the following common teenage situations.

Generalization

Thought: *Popular teenagers at school are rude when you try to talk to them.*

This thought can make you avoid being friendly to potentially amazing people at your school or in your neighborhood and make you feel angry or defensive when you are around them. You can challenge this generalization through a new way of thinking.

Challenge: *A person's nature is what makes them rude, not their popularity.*

This will help you keep an open mind and recognize body language cues from popular teenagers that invite friendly inter-actions.

A Friend Doesn't Show Up to Your Party

Thought: They're a fake friend.

Feelings: betrayal and anger.

Belief: that your friend doesn't care about you.

When your friend approaches you the next day and tells you a story of why they didn't show up, you can tell that they feel bad about not showing up to the party but also that the story is a lie. Even if you self-regulated through the initial anger, this sense of being deceived can bring those feelings back up again. In fact, this feeling likely intensifies because of the additional level of betrayal.

However, instead of giving in to the negative feeling, you start using CBT restructuring by considering other possible valid reasons why your friend didn't show up at your party— perhaps, something awful happened to a family member, and your friend is only lying to protect their privacy. By considering other alternatives, you can help the feelings of anger and betrayal subside and be complemented by your compassionate feelings of concern over why your friend feels bad and thinks they need to lie to you. You can empathetically communicate your disappointment without accusation and assure them that they can tell you why they didn't show up.

Then, if your friend sighs and tells you that they have social anxiety, you might immediately feel sorry for them, but using the techniques you learned, CBT can change the feelings of pity to feelings of hope that your friend can overcome their anxiety. To help them feel safe in their vulnerability with you, you could even decide to tell them about the effectiveness of CBT, how you used to feel, and how you have used it to control your overwhelming emotions.

Building the Habit

Once you create the habit of using CBT techniques in your everyday life, you will be able to carry out the processes without the need to consciously remember each step. In the same way that Einstein's words say that in order not to fall off a bicycle you must keep moving, the following techniques can help you to create a habit of using CBT.

- **Set a schedule:** While some CBT skills are more suited to be used in the moment, setting a schedule makes it easier for you to be consistent with the practice of using CBT techniques, as a whole. You can incorporate regular use of introspection or reflection techniques like writing down how you feel and the thoughts you have.
- **Use reminders and apps:** In addition to relieving your stress by managing your time, reminders on your smartphone can be used for integrating your CBT schedule into your daily life. The reminders will help you to effectively manage other activities before the time to practice CBT begins, freeing up your mind to truly engage with the techniques. It is also best to consider downloading and using CBT-specific apps like

Happify or Bloom; each of these apps is designed to meet a specific CBT outcome.

CREATING A CBT TOOLKIT

Creating a CBT toolkit is easy: First, you must recognize your immediate need—for instance, to overcome your fears of an upcoming test—and then plan based on the CBT techniques and knowledge that you have gathered from this book. Technological assistance can come in handy, but there are so many CBT apps out there that the process of finding the right one might seem challenging. Keep in mind that the "right" app doesn't have to be perfect; it's simply one that is capable of meeting your immediate needs.

Using flashcards as visual reminders of the CBT techniques at your disposal has also been proven to be effective; this is not only because they are a convenient memory cue but also because the process of creating flashcards is very much like journaling—allowing you to emotionally process the need to use the skills; except that you are also adding fun pictures, colors, and special objects or symbols to the writing, making it particularly effective for internalizing new information. Flashcards also increase your ability to be mindfully present as touching and seeing the flashcards stimulates your senses, grounding you in the here and now. This creative process will also enable you to take a new perspective on any issue.

Personalize Your Toolkit

You can personalize your CBT toolkit by making adjustments to the combinations of tools like apps, flashcards, journals, journaling prompts, or any other tool that you may think will be more specific to your needs and goals—such as an achievement resume if you are aiming to improve your self-esteem. Keep in mind that the design of your toolkit should be focused on your immediate needs rather than your desired results. This will give you a much wider perspective on how the CBT tools can be used; the bottom line is to remember that just because a tool is not effective at dealing with one particular issue doesn't mean that it's useless for other circumstances that you may come across as a teenager. Let a growth mindset lead you through the process of experimentation with CBT tools.

Consistency Is Key

Consistency has already been emphasized and encouraged throughout this book. Using a calendar and setting reminders on your smartphone can help you to stay consistent. Focus on the process rather than the results, and if you think you need to reach out to an expert to get you started on the use of CBT and incorporating it into your daily life, then do; it's not about *how* you get started but that you *do* get started.

Activities

You can add the following exercises to your toolkit and modify them as needed to make your CBT usage more diverse.

Understanding Anxiety

With what you have learned so far about anxiety, on a scale of 1 to 10, how comfortable are you telling your friends at school or in the neighborhood about it? Note: Telling your friends is *not* part of the exercise; just work on identifying your internal reaction to the idea of talking to them about your emotions. Use journaling to reflect on any negative feelings or thoughts that you might have, and use CBT techniques to change them.

Getting Comfortable With Outcomes That Are Less Satisfactory

Consider how you would feel if you were a top-performing member of your drama class; think about the experience of no longer getting stage fright whenever taking on a new act. Then, visualize that when the school play is cast, someone else is chosen for the lead role; you are cast as a supporting actor. Observe the emotions and limiting beliefs that rise in response to this disappointment. Evaluate, on a scale of 1 to 10, how comfortable you would be taking on a minor supporting role in this context. Reflect on why you would feel any level of discomfort, and explore the CBT techniques you would use to regulate your way through these emotions if you encountered a similar disappointment. Determine what skills you can use in the meantime to build your emotional resilience.

Dealing With a Blow to Your Self-Esteem

Visualize the following: On Valentine's Day, everyone in your school starts posting TikToks of their dates; a tagging cyberbullying trend starts, making fun of people without a Valentine's date. Then, one of your classmates tags you in a comment on the trend, and more of your classmates respond with laughing emojis. On a scale of 1 to 10, how heavily would your self-esteem be affected? What insecurities or limiting beliefs would an experience like this trigger? Explore how you can use the CBT tips from the earlier chapters to build your self-esteem.

Dealing With Friendship Dramas

Imagine that you are in the school cafeteria, making your way to your friends who are sitting at a table heavily engaged in a conversation when one of them makes an obvious gesture for everyone to stop talking and change the topic. Then, they all turn their attention to you with faux-friendly smiles, asking how your day was. On a scale of 1 to 10, how comfortable would you be with addressing or ignoring what just happened? Explore how you can use the CBT techniques to prevent thoughts like, Why didn't they want me to hear what they were saying? or to assertively communicate that you'd like to know what was going on without accusing your friends of behaving rudely and causing reactive defensiveness.

You're an Inspiration!

You're ready to embark on a transformative journey – and that puts you in the perfect position to inspire someone else to take the same road.

Simply by sharing your honest opinion of this book and a little about your own experience, you'll show new readers where they can find all the skills they need to conquer the chaos and step forward into a happy and confident future.

LEAVE A REVIEW!

Thank you so much for your support! I wish you every success with putting your new skills into practice.

Scan the QR code below to leave your review.

CONCLUSION

As you reflect back on where you were before reading this book, you may find that simply knowing there are ways to manage your emotions eases your anxiety about your teenage years. You now have a clear understanding that you are not alone. In fact, most teenagers are in the same emotional boat; but you are lucky enough to know that you don't have to keep feeling so overwhelmed.

This book has given you the tools that will help you navigate through your teen life with ease. Take some time to reflect on how the teenage brain works and the implications this has on your thoughts. Remember that with the right CBT techniques, you will anticipate the effects of the surges of your hormones, have compassion for your ever-changing brain, and be capable of working out effective mood-regulating strategies.

You know that most misconceptions about teenagers and societal expectations come from misguided conclusions and you can, therefore, cut yourself some slack about not being able to be "perfect."

Your successes with using CBT can come from outlining your plans through the use of SMART goal strategies. They give you a strong sense of commitment and an adequately prepared foundation to achieve change. You may find that these successes attract friends at school, as your improved self-worth and communication skills make developing and maintaining teenage friendships much easier, especially when you are also trying to figure yourself out and have enough time for educational commitments. Stress is expected, but by applying the techniques that you have learned throughout this book, you will be able to use effective strategies to not just survive your teen years but thrive through them.

But the key here is turning theory into practice. Knowing that CBT can help is only the first step; now, it's up to you to train that brain of yours to be nicer to you!

With awareness of yourself and the common sources of stress for people your age, you will anticipate some peer pressure and be able to recognize its many different forms. Rather than sinking into self-pity or aggressively confronting your friends when you catch them trying to get you to do something that you are not comfortable with, CBT techniques will help you to assertively stick to your values. Commonly used advice tells a lot of teenagers to completely cut off friends that may try to negatively influence them, but by extending empathy to yourself and your peers, you will recognize that this way of thinking fails to account for the fact that many teenagers may not even know that they are engaging in peer pressure. So, rather than falling into the trap of the hot-and-cold, push-and-pull of holding unrealistic expectations for your friends, you will remain steady, knowing the power and importance of friendships and, most importantly, that your use of CBT techniques will protect you from peer pressure.

Likewise, no one should stop using the internet and social media just because of the negative influences and effects it has. CBT teaches us how to engage in moderation by using techniques to be safe from a wide variety of social media threats. This book has outlined the types of cyberbullying with practical solutions to build resilience against their adverse effects. By following this guidance, you will maintain a steadying influence over your thoughts and emotions, even if you become super active on social media. Additionally, you may even inspire some of your friends to join you in your approach to using social media.

However, you must also remember that building resilience is about more than your digital life because the real world has enough troubles of its own that can negatively impact your feelings. Refer back to the strategies on how to build emotional resilience, and recognize why this is important. Try to reflect on the understanding you have acquired of how emotional resilience works and how it can be built or strengthened by using the 7Cs—confidence, competence, connections, character, contributions, coping, and control. Additionally, as you have come to understand, emotional intelligence goes hand in hand with emotional resilience; so, by using emotional resilience exercises—such as journaling, using grounding techniques, and mindfulness—and building a support structure, you cannot only manage your own emotions effectively but also communicate empathetically with others.

As you continue to effectively navigate through your life, your confidence will continue to grow. But things never stay the same, and the transitional period to adulthood is a very important stage. As we discussed in Chapter 7, this period is usually marked by the idea of the permanence of things such as the career you will have, the mistakes that can't be fixed, and the failures that might repeat themselves over and over again during your adult life. It's particularly easy to be absorbed by these fears if you are concerned that your current, unhealthy standard of living may continue. Conversely, it's also very easy to ruminate on future fears if you have had a relatively low-pressure life up to this point, therefore making independence seem like too large a leap to be achievable. Many people who give in to this fear end up experiencing what has been called *failure to launch*. By modeling the use of CBT skills in front of your friends, you can be a pillar of healthy norms and advice for any teenagers who develop anxieties during this period, offering them the information you have learned on how to unpack future anxieties. These techniques will also reduce your own worrying and help you to stay mindfully present.

As you become more comfortable with using CBT techniques, your confidence will undoubtedly blossom. Confidence is a very powerful asset when building the foundation of your future. Even in your adult years, it is important to continue to build it through the techniques that you have read in this book; lucky you, getting a head start on things most people don't learn until at least their twenties! Use mirror talks to build your self-worth and confidence, build positive affirmation routines in your daily life, and adopt a growth mindset. This will develop, maintain, and continue to increase your confidence, empowering you to keep reaching more and more achievements.

As you have come to realize, your teenage years are a wonderful stage of life that you can make use of on your journey to reach your dreams. Whatever circumstances you are in today—no matter what other people have told you, preventing you from having the hope to dream, explore, and fully enjoy the great times of your teenage life—you can overcome all of these things with the use of CBT.

CBT is specifically focused on the interconnectedness of your thoughts, behaviors, and emotions, making it a realistic and practical technique for changing your life. As you were reading, you started the practice of CBT; the only thing left for you to do is to continue by creating a scheduled routine for using the various techniques explained in this book.

Your mental health is in your hands! You can build your support network along this journey through social media posts, text messages, and CBT groups and help others find this amazing source of relief by telling people about your experience of reading this book and leaving a review.

Good luck, friend, on your continued CBT journey!

REFERENCES

Abrams, Z. (2023, August 3). *Why young brains are especially vulnerable to social media.* American Psychology Association. https://www.apa.org/news/apa/2022/social-media-children-teens

Aiken, C. (2020, October 26). *Overthinking, worry, and rumination.* Psych Education. https://psycheducation.org/blog/overthinking-worry-and-rumination/

Aletheia. (2022, November 16). *How to practice mirror work (7 step guide).* Loner Wolf. https://lonerwolf.com/mirror-work-guide/

Anderson, M., Vogels, A, E., Perrin, A., Raine, L. (2022, November 16). *Connection, creativity and drama: Teen life on social media in 2022.* Pew Research Center https://www.pewresearch.org/internet/2022/11/16/connection-creativity-and-drama-teen-life-on-social-media-in-2022/

Anxiety and brain. (n.d). Direct. https://directindia.org/resources/anxiety-and-the-brain/

Anxiety and panic attacks. (n.d). Mind. https://www.mind.org.uk/information-support/types-of-mental-health-problems/anxiety-and-panic-attacks/symptoms/

Anxiety disorders. (2023, January 7). WebMD. https://www.webmd.com/anxiety-panic/anxiety-disorders

Anxiety Disorders - Facts & statistics. (n.d). Anxiety & Depression Association of America. https://adaa.org/understanding-anxiety/facts-statistics

Anxiety. (n.d). Medline Plus. https://medlineplus.gov/anxiety.html

Anxiety on the rise among the young in social media age. (n.d). The Guardian. https://www.theguardian.com/society/2019/feb/05/youth-unhappiness-uk-doubles-in-past-10-years

Arwine, A. (2023, September 22). *Cognitive bahavioral therapy for teens - A complete guide.* Clear ForK Academy. https://clearforkacademy.com/blog/cognitive-behavioral-therapy-for-teens-a-complete-guide/

Asiendu-Kwatchey, E. (2022, August 10). *Influencer culture: The creator. Mindless Magazine.* https://www.mindlessmag.com/post/is-influencer-culture-driving-unrealistic-beauty-standards

Atta, S. (2023, August 16). *Perspective and boost your mood.* Medium. https://

sampreetiatta.medium.com/how-changing-your-thought-patterns-can-transform-your-perspective-and-boost-your-mood-75b260f73410

Avoidance. (n.d). Anxiety Canada. https://www.anxietycanada.com/articles/avoidance/

Avoiding overcommitment. (n.d). American Psychology Association. https://www.apa.org/gradpsych/2005/11/matters

Babauta, L. (n.d). *5 powerful reasons to make reflection a daily habit, and how to do it.* Zen Habits. https://zenhabits.net/5-powerful-reasons-to-make-reflection-a-daily-habit-and-how-to-do-it/

Bailey, E. (2010, September 7). *What is "Fight or Flight" and how does it relate to anxiety?* Health Central. https://www.healthcentral.com/article/what-is-fight-or-flight-and-how-does-it-relate-to-anxiety

Bailey R, R. (2017, September 13). *Goal setting and action plan for health behavior change.* National Library of Medicine. https://www.ncbi.nlm.nih.gov/pmc/articles/PMC6796229/

Barnhart, B. (2023, June 8). *7 steps for prioritizing your workload.* Team Work. https://www.teamwork.com/blog/how-to-prioritize-tasks/

Barr, S. (2022, January 19). *Six ways social media negatively affects your mental health. Independent.* https://www.independent.co.uk/life-style/health-and-families/social-media-mental-health-anxiety-b1996486.html

Bell, C. (2022, April 7). *15 Best CBT Apps of 2022.* Choosing Therapy. https://www.choosingtherapy.com/best-cbt-apps/

Benefits of mindfulness. (n.d). Help Guide. https://www.helpguide.org/harvard/benefits-of-mindfulness.htm

Benisek, A. (2022, September 2). *Depression and anxiety: Are they hereditary?* WebMD. https://www.webmd.com/depression/are-depression-anxiety-hereditary

Bhatnager, S. (2022, October 19). *Deep dive into CBT tools and techniques.* Medium. https://sampada-bhatnagar.medium.com/deep-dive-into-cbt-tools-and-techniques-ff7b40a5571f

Brain development in pre-teens and teenagers. (n.d). Raising Children. https://raisingchildren.net.au/pre-teens/development/understanding-your-pre-teen/brain-development-teens

Brewer, B. (2023, January 13). *Why teens and young adults suffer from the phobia of growing up.* Charlie Health. https://www.charliehealth.com/post/why-teens-and-young-adults-suffer-from-a-phobia-of-growing-up

Brown, D. (2019, December 19). *Remember Vine? These social networking sites defined the past decade.* USA Today. https://www.usatoday.com/story/tech/2019/12/19/end-decade-heres-how-social-media-has-evolved-over-10-years/4227619002/#:

Building a community around mental health - finding a support system for your teen. (2017, September 8). Polaris Teen Center. https://polaristeen.com/articles/building-community-around-mental-health/

Cantor, E. (2022, June 2). *Dealing with loneliness as a young adult.* Choosing Therapy. https://www.choosingtherapy.com/loneliness-young-adult/

Capps, R. (2023, June 20). *The benefits of daily self-reflection for your well-being.* Montecito Journal. https://www.montecitojournal.net/2023/06/20/the-benefits-of-daily-self-reflection-for-your-well-being/

Carnevale, J. (n.d). *What is peer pressure?* Study.Com. https://study.com/learn/lesson/what-is-peer-pressure.html

Carrico, B. (2021. July 19). *What is emotional invalidation?* Psych Central. https://psychcentral.com/health/reasons-you-and-others-invalidate-your-emotional-experience

Catch it. Check it. Change it. (n.d). BBC. http://downloads.bbc.co.uk/headroom/cbt/catch_it.pdf

CBT for teens: How cognitive behavioral therapy works. (2022, October 1). NewPort Academy. https://www.newportacademy.com/resources/mental-health/cbt-treatment/

Challenging negative thinking with Socratic questioning by Rachel Funnel, LMFT. (2020, December 13). Parent and Child Psychology Services. https://www.childtherapysrq.com/blog/challenging-negative-thinking-with-socratic-questioning-by-rachel-funnell-lmft

Changing your outlook: How CBT works. (n.d). Destination Hope Treatment Center. https://destinationhope.com/changing-your-outlook-how-cbt-works/

Chen, A. (2017, August 26). *Having a best friend in your teenage years could benefit you for life.* NPR. https://www.npr.org/sections/health-shots/2017/08/26/543739986/having-a-best-friend-in-your-teenage-years-could-benefit-you-for-life

Cherry, K. (2023, April 14). *How to deal with the fear of failure.* Very Well Mind. https://www.verywellmind.com/what-is-the-fear-of-failure-5176202

Cherry, K. (2023, May 2). *Emotional intelligence: How we perceive, evaluate, express, and control emotions.* Very Well Mind. https://www.verywellmind.com/what-is-emotional-intelligence-2795423

Cirino, E. (2023, October 19). *12 tips to help you stop ruminating.* Healthline. https://www.healthline.com/health/how-to-stop-ruminating

Claney, D. (2023, July 18). *Understanding how hormonal changes impact emotional health for teens.* Relational Psych. https://www.relationalpsych.group/arti cles/understanding-how-hormonal-changes-impact-emotional-health-for-teens

CBT techniques: Cognitive and behavioral. (2014, November 5). Counselling Connection. https://www.counsellingconnection.com/index.php/2014/11/05/cbt-techniques-cognitive-and-behavioural/

Cognitive behavioral therapy (CBT) and role play techniques. (n.d). Grouport. https://www.grouporttherapy.com/blog/cognitive-behavioral-therapy-role-play

Cognitive behavioral therapy. (n.d). Mayo Clinic. https://www.mayoclinic.org/tests-procedures/cognitive-behavioral-therapy/about/pac-20384610

Cognitive development in the teen years. (n.d). Stanford Medicine. https://www.stanfordchildrens.org/en/topic/default?id=cognitive-development-90-P01594

Common misconceptions about anxiety disorders. (n.d). Banyan. https://www.banyanmentalhealth.com/2018/08/02/common-misconceptions-about-anxiety-disorders/

Confidence in pre-teens and teenagers. (n.d). Raising Children. https://raisingchil dren.net.au/pre-teens/development/social-emotional-development/confi dence-in-teens

Conniff, M. (2022, February 7). *Too much homework causes overload in teens.* The Valhalla. https://lshsvalhalla.com/opinion/too-much-homework-causes-overload-in-teens/

Coping with setbacks. (2011, August 20). KMA Therapy. https://www.kmather apy.com/blog/cognitive-therapycoping-setbacks

Core beliefs in CBT - Identifying and analyzing your personal beliefs. (1970, January 1). Harley Therapy. https://www.harleytherapy.co.uk/coun selling/core-beliefs-cbt.htm

Core beliefs in cognitive behavioural Therapy (CBT). (n.d). Guelph Therapist. https://www.guelphtherapist.ca/blog/core-beliefs-in-cognitive-therapy-cognitive-behavioural-therapy-cbt/

Cornetti, M. (2015, October 13). *The five most common self-limiting beliefs.* LinkedIn. https://www.linkedin.com/pulse/five-most-common-self-limit ing-beliefs-monica-cornetti-lion-/

Crosby, J. (2023, October 23). *What is self-reflection & how to reflect.* Thrive Works. https://thriveworks.com/blog/importance-self-reflection-improvement/

Crossfield, A. (2020, November 3). *Is your teen anxious about change and growing up?* Psychology Today. https://www.psychologytoday.com/ca/blog/emotionally-healthy-teens/202011/is-your-teen-anxious-about-change-and-growing

Cuncic, A. (2023, February 13). *How to stop negative thoughts.* Very Well Mind. https://www.verywellmind.com/how-to-change-negative-thinking-3024843

Developing critical thinking in teens. (n.d). Reboot. https://reboot-foundation.org/parent-guide/ages-13-plus/

Deyo, J. (2023, April 6). *TikTok remains top social app for teens despite drop in favorability, study finds.* Marketing Dive. https://www.marketingdive.com/news/tiktok-social-marketing-teens-snap-instagram-piper-sandler/646930/

Drew, C. (2023, September 8). *30 Self-reflection examples.* Helpful Professor. https://helpfulprofessor.com/self-reflection-examples/

Duarte, F. (2023, November 10). *Average screen time for teens (2024).* Exploding Topics. https://explodingtopics.com/blog/screen-time-for-teens

Economy, P. (2019, May 22). *The very best mirror affirmations for confidence and success beyond what you ever.* Inc Africa. https://www.incafrica.com/library/peter-economy-the-vbest-mirror-affirmations-for-confidence-success-beyond-what-you-ever-imagined

8 resources both online and in-person to help teens with anxiety. (2023, October 31). Better Help. https://www.betterhelp.com/advice/teenagers/helping-teens-with-anxiety-8-resources-both-online-and-in-person/

11 real issues that teens face every day. (2021, August 16). A Brighter Day. https://abrighterday.info/11-real-issues-that-teens-face-every-day/

Emotional Resilience: How to build emotional resilience. (2022, May 26). Master Class. https://www.masterclass.com/articles/emotional-resilience

Empowering self-reflection with cognitive behavioral therapy journal prompts: ideas and examples. (n.d). Grouport. https://www.grouporttherapy.com/blog/cbt-journal-prompts

Failure to launch syndrome: How to help teens and young adults. (n.d). Embark Behavioral Health. https://www.embarkbh.com/blog/failure-to-launch-syndrome/

Failure to launch syndrome. (n.d). Optimum Performance Institute. https://www.optimumperformanceinstitute.com/failure-to-launch-syndrome/

Felman, A. (2023, October 8). *What to know about anxiety.* Medical News Today. https://www.medicalnewstoday.com/articles/323454

Ferguson, S. (206, December 22). *4 harmful ways we dismiss teenagers' mental health issues.* Everyday Feminism. https://everydayfeminism.com/2016/12/dismiss-teenagers-mental-health/

Fiden, B. (2021, April 9). *Does social media create an unrealistic standard of happiness?* In Flow Network. https://inflownetwork.com/does-social-media-create-an-unrealistic-standard-of-happiness/

15 core CBT techniques you can use right now. (n.d). Mark Tyrrell's Therapy Skills. https://www.unk.com/blog/15-core-cbt-techniques-you-can-use-right-now/

50 tips for improving your emotional intelligence. (n.d). Roche Martin. https://www.rochemartin.com/blog/50-tips-improving-emotional-intelligence5 grounding techniques for adolescents with anxiety disorder.* (2017, April 3). Polaris Teen Center. https://polaristeen.com/articles/grounding-excercises-teen-anxiety/https://polaristeen.com/articles/grounding-excercises-teen-anxiety/

5 journaling prompts for self-reflection and discovery. (2022, May 26). Evernote. https://evernote.com/blog/journal-prompts-self-reflection-discovery

Flashcards. (n.d), Central Penn College. https://guides.centralpenn.edu/c.php?g=695569&p=4999857

Folk, J. (2021, May 19). *Sensory overload.* Anxiety Centre. https://www.anxietycentre.com/anxiety-disorders/symptoms/sensory-overload-anxiety/

Frew, J. (2023, February 11). *11 CBT group therapy activity ideas with examples.* Care Patron. https://www.carepatron.com/blog/11-cbt-group-therapy-activity-ideas-with-examples

Friends: Quality over quantity is what counts. (n.d). Cheers to Chapter Two. https://cheers2chapter2.com/friends-quality-over-quantity-is-what-counts

Generalized anxiety disorder. (n.d). Mayo Clinic. https://www.mayoclinic.org/diseases-conditions/generalized-anxiety-disorder/symptoms-causes/syc-20360803

Generalized anxiety disorder: When worry gets out of control. (n.d). National Institute of Mental Health. https://www.nimh.nih.gov/health/publications/generalized-anxiety-disorder-gad

Gayde, L. (2018, June 29). *What part of the brain deals with anxiety? What can brains affected by anxiety tell us?* Brain Facts. https://www.brainfacts.org/diseases-and-disorders/mental-health/2018/what-part-of-the-brain-deals-with-anxiety-what-can-brains-affected-by-anxiety-tell-us-062918

Giedd, N, J. (2016, May 1). *The amazing teen brain.* Scientific American. https://www.scientificamerican.com/article/the-amazing-teen-brain/

Gillison, Ben, and Catherine Pulsifer. "56 Quotes About Inspiring Others – Wow4u." Wow4u – Inspirational Words of Wisdom. Last modified March 13, 2023. https://www.wow4u.com/56-quotes-about-inspiring-others/

Ginsburg, K. (2018, September 4). *Building Resilience: The 7 Cs.* Strengthening Family Connections. https://parentandteen.com/building-resilience-in-teens/

Goal setting in therapy. (2020, December 21). Taylor Counseling Group. https://taylorcounselinggroup.com/blog/goal-setting-in-therapy/

Goldman, R. (2022, November 4). *Affirmations: What they are, health benefits, and getting started.* Everyday Health. https://www.everydayhealth.com/emotional-health/what-are-affirmations/

Growth mindset: Develop the confidence to succeed. (n.d). The Big Bang Partnership. https://bigbangpartnership.co.uk/growth-mindset/

Grupe, W, D., Nitschke, B, J. (2013, July 14). *Uncertainty and anticipation in anxiety.* National Library of Medicine. https://www.ncbi.nlm.nih.gov/pmc/articles/PMC4276319/

Gupta, S. (2033, May 26). *The importance of self-reflection: How looking inward can improve your mental health.* Very Well Mind. https://www.verywellmind.com/self-reflection-importance-benefits-and-strategies-7500858

Guyer, E, A., Silk, S, J. (2016, August 6). *The neurobiology of emotional adolescent: From the inside out.* National Library of Medicine. https://www.ncbi.nlm.nih.gov/pmc/articles/PMC5074886/

Hill, S. (2023, August 24). *Why is school so stressful? Exploring causes and solutions.* Healium. https://www.tryhealium.com/2023/08/24/why-is-school-so-stressful/

Hillier, C. (2021, November 18). *Unfiltered: Teens get real about the fake lives lived on social media.* CBC. https://www.cbc.ca/news/canada/newfoundland-labrador/unfiltered-teens-social-media-1.6250963

Hippe, H. (2023, January 13). *6 tips to build authentic connections.* Nystrom & Associates. https://www.nystromcounseling.com/relationships/6-tips-to-build-authentic-connections/

Hitching, G. (n.d). *What is assertiveness?* Science of People. https://www.scienceofpeople.com/stand-up-for-yourself/

Hoffower, H. (2019, July 1). *How teen friendships shape your mental health as a young adult.* Business Insider Africa. https://africa.businessinsider.com/life style/how-teen-friendships-shape-your-mental-health-as-a-young-adult/6tmd5zq

Hoshaw, C. (2022, May 2). *The benefits of social media break, plus 30 things to do instead.* Healthline. https://www.healthline.com/health/mental-health/the-benefits-of-a-social-media-break-plus-30-things-to-do-instead

How are emotional intelligence and resilience connected? (2016, April 2). Mindful Solutions. http://www.drcarlamessenger.com/moving-forward-blog/2016/4/11/how-are-emotional-intelligence-and-resilience-connected

How does anxiety affect cognitive ability? (2022, December 27). Amen Clinics. https://www.amenclinics.com/blog/how-does-anxiety-affect-cognitive-ability/

How do "likes" affect the well-being of teens? (2021, July 27). Harmony. https://www.grwhealth.com/post/how-do-likes-affect-the-well-being-of-teens-2/

How mindfulness builds resilience: What science says. (n.d.). Mindfulness Exercises. https://mindfulnessexercises.com/how-mindfulness-builds-resilience-what-science-says/

How to build and maintain a strong support system for teenagers. (2018, January 23). Paradigm Treatment. https://paradigmtreatment.com/build-main tain-strong-support-system/

How to break negative thought patterns with CBT techniques. (2023, May 8). ASIC. https://www.asicrecoveryservices.com/post/break-negative-thought-patterns

How to build effective relationships as a teenager. (2023, January 20). Back On Track Teens. https://www.backontrackteens.com/blog/build-effective-relationships-as-teenager/

How to journal for mental clarity: Master the power of reflection. (2023, May 17). Cognifit. https://blog.cognifit.com/how-to-journal-for-mental-clarity-master-the-power-of-reflection/

How to make SMART goals. (n.d.). HPA Live Well. https://hpalivewell.com/how-to-make-smart-goals/

How to set boundaries and limit screen time. (2021, May 12). Merrimack Valley Psychology associates. https://www.mvpsych.com/blog/limit-screen-time/

How your environment affects your mental health. (n.d). National Counselling Society. https://nationalcounsellingsociety.org/blog/posts/how-your-envi ronment-affects-your-mental-health

Hurley, K. (2022, July 14). *What is resilience? Your guide to facing life's challenges, adversities, and crises.* Everyday Health. https://www.everydayhealth.com/ wellness/resilience/

Introspection - Definition, psychology, and applications. (2023, January 4). Better-lylyf. https://www.betterlyf.com/articles/self-esteem-and-confidence/ introspection

Introspection in psychology: Meaning, method, uses, and limitations. (2022, May 27). The Pleasant Mind. https://thepleasantmind.com/introspection-in-psychology/

Is being popular at school really that important. (2010, January 5). Kids At Risk. https://kidsatrisk.wordpress.com/tag/the-pros-and-cons-being-popular-at-school/

Jerome, W, L. (2022, December 23). *How to recognize negative thought cycles and stop obsessing.* Psychology Today. https://www.psychologytoday.com/ca/ blog/the-stories-we-tell/202212/how-to-recognize-negative-thought-loops-and-stop-obsessing

Josefowitz, N. (2017, August 28). *Popularity: The advantages and disadvantages, status versus congeniality.* Huff Post. https://www.huffpost.com/entry/popu larity-the-advantages-and-disadvantages-status_b_59a491e5e4b03c5da162aef0

Joy, R. (2023, June 5). *How to change negative thinking with constructive restruc-turing.* Healthline. https://www.healthline.com/health/cognitive-restruc turing#how-does-it-work

Kaminsky, A. (2016, September 27). *Teens, social media and the illusion of perfec-tion.* Advanced Psychology Services. https://www.psy-ed.com/wpblog/ teens-and-social-media/

Kesarovska, L. (2023, July 7). *20 powerful mirror affirmations for confidence using the mirror technique.* Lets Reach Success. https://letsreachsuccess.com/ mirror-affirmations/

Keelan, P. (n.d). *CBT across the life span: How it works for clients of different ages.* Dr. Patrick Keelan. https://drpatrickkeelan.com/psychology/cbt-across-the-life-span-how-it-works-for-clients-of-different-ages/

Keelan, P. (n.d). *Change your thinking to manage your emotions.* Dr. Patrick

Keelan.   https://drpatrickkeelan.com/depression/change-thinking-manage-emotions-behaviours/

Kerslake, R. (2021, September 20). *Everything you need to know about cognitive behavioral therapy for anxiety.* Healthline. https://www.healthline.com/health/anxiety/cbt-for-anxiety

Kris, F, D. (2019, February 12). *How to help teenage girls reframe anxiety and strengthen resilience.* KQED. https://www.kqed.org/mindshift/52994/how-to-help-teenage-girls-reframe-anxiety-and-strengthen-resilience

Kulkarni, J. (2015. October 1). *Chemical messengers: how hormones affect our mood.* The Conversation. https://theconversation.com/chemical-messengers-how-hormones-affect-our-mood-42422

Landou, C. (n.d). *16 effective prioritization and time management strategies.* Hour Stack. https://hourstack.com/blog/16-effective-prioritization-and-time-management-strategies

Lee, Y, H., Jamieson, P, J., Reis, T, H., Beevers, G, C., Josephs A, R., Mullarkey, C, M., O'Brien, J., Yeager, S, D. (2021, November 1). *Getting fewer "likes" than others on social media elicits emotional distress among victimized adolescents.* National Library of Medicine. https://www.ncbi.nlm.nih.gov/pmc/articles/PMC7722198/

Levy, S. (2019, August 22). *Is too much homework bad for kids' health?* Healthline. https://www.healthline.com/health-news/children-more-homework-means-more-stress-031114

Lockett, E. (2023, March 15). *Breaking the cycle of anxiety and avoidance.* Healthline.   https://www.healthline.com/health/anxiety/anxiety-avoidance

Lukin, K. (n.d). *5 surprising effective cognitive behavioral therapy exercises.* Lukin Center. https://www.lukincenter.com/5-surprisingly-effective-cognitive-behavioral-therapy-exercises/

Makowski, M. (2020, December 1). *What is cognitive flexibility and how do I help my child with it?* Foothills Academy. https://www.foothillsacademy.org/community/articles/cognitive-flexibility

Marr, B. (2023, June 9). *Picture perfect: The hidden consequences of AI beauty filters.* Forbes. https://www.forbes.com/sites/bernardmarr/2023/06/09/picture-perfect-the-hidden-consequences-of-ai-beauty-filters/?sh=1481e0187d5d

Marrs, T. *5 ways to help your teen create a support system.* (n.d). Finding Solutions. https://create.dibbly.com/d/d5VZnLBsBT3KBvaiUb0q

Marschall, A. (2022, June 2). *Is Anxiety Genetic?* Very Well Mind. https://www.verywellmind.com/is-anxiety-genetic-5271575

Matud, P, M., Diaz, A., Bethencourt., J, M., Ibanez, I. (2020, September 4). *Stress and psychology distress in emerging adulthood: A gender analysis.* National Library of Medicine. https://www.ncbi.nlm.nih.gov/pmc/articles/PMC7564698/

Mbanza, A. (n.d). *When you fear making the "wrong" decision.* Tinny Buddha. https://tinybuddha.com/blog/when-you-fear-making-the-wrong-decision/

Monaghan, J. (2023, September 20). *Turning setbacks into stepping stones: Using challenges as motivation to achieve your life's goals.* LinkedIn. https://www.linkedin.com/pulse/turning-setbacks-stepping-stones-using-challenges-achieve-monaghan/

Moore, M. (2022, June 23). *Mindfulness: The art of cultivating resilience.* Psych Central. https://psychcentral.com/lib/mindfulness-the-art-of-cultivating-resilience

Morin, A. (2021. July 11). *Are my teenager's rapid mood swings normal?* Very Well Family. https://www.verywellfamily.com/are-my-teens-mood-swings-normal-2611240

Morin, A. (2022, September 20). *10 social issues and problems that trouble today's teens.* Very Well Family. https://www.verywellfamily.com/startling-facts-about-todays-teenagers-2608914

Naar, S. (2021, July 26). *The transition from adolescence to adulthood.* Psychology Today. https://www.psychologytoday.com/ca/blog/metamorphosis/202107/the-transition-adolescence-adulthood

Parental expectations - 5 ways these can cause your child to be anxious. (n.d). Anxious Child Help. https://www.anxiouschildhelp.com/parental-expectations.html

Parent's expectations and academic pressure: A major cause of stress among students. (2020, November 30). India Today. https://www.indiatoday.in/education-today/featurephilia/story/parent-s-expectations-and-academic-pressure-a-major-cause-of-stress-among-students-1743857-2020-11-25

Main, P. (2023, April 28). *Cognitive behavior therapy techniques.* Structural Learning. https://www.structural-learning.com/post/cognitive-behavior-therapy-techniques

Mandriota, M. (2022, June 30). *7 mindfulness exercises for teens and tips to get started.* Psych Central. https://psychcentral.com/health/the-benefits-of-mindfulness-meditation-for-teens

Marksman, A. (2011, August 12). *Your view of the future is shaped by the past.* Psychology Today. https://www.psychologytoday.com/ca/blog/ulterior-motives/201108/your-view-the-future-is-shaped-the-past

McClung, J. (2015, March 19). *5 ways to maintain balance between work, school, and life.* Way Up. https://www.wayup.com/guide/community/5-ways-to-maintain-balance-between-work-school-and-life/

Menon, A. *Career anxieties among teenagers.* Lifelogy Magazine. https://magazine.lifology.com/career/career-anxieties-among-teenagers/

Mirror healing and the 5 powerful benefits. (2021, November 9). Mal Paper. https://malpaper.com/blogs/news/mirror-healing-and-the-powerful-benefits

Morin, A. (2021, February 20). *8 essential strategies for raising a confident teen.* Very Well Family. https://www.verywellfamily.com/essential-strategies-for-raising-a-confident-teen-2611002

Most teens really do want to fit in... here's why. (n.d). Raising Teens Today. https://raisingteenstoday.com/most-teens-really-do-want-to-fit-in-heres-why/

9 best CBT therapy apps in 2023. (n.d). Care Patron. https://www.carepatron.com/app/cbt-therapy-apps

9 common myths about anxiety. (2023, May 8). The Recovery Village. https://www.therecoveryvillage.com/mental-health/anxiety/anxiety-myths/

Parsons, L. (2022, October 14). *8 time management tips for students.* Harvard Summer School. https://summer.harvard.edu/blog/8-time-management-tips-for-students/

PART 2: Getting started with CBT: Setting goals. (n.d). Cognitive Behavioral Therapy Los Angeles. https://cogbtherapy.com/setting-goals-in-cbt

Part 6: Cognitive restructuring to change your thinking. (n.d). Cognitive Behavioral Therapy Los Angeles. https://cogbtherapy.com/cognitive-restructuring-in-cbt

Patalano, G. (n.d) *Surprising ways anxiety can manifest.* My Well Being. https://mywellbeing.com/therapy-101/surprising-ways-anxiety-can-manifest

Peper, J, S., Dahl E, R. ((2013. April 22). *Surging Hormones: Brain-Behavior Interactions During Puberty.* National Library of Medicine. https://www.ncbi.nlm.nih.gov/pmc/articles/PMC4539143/

Peer pressure. (n.d). Kids Health. https://kidshealth.org/en/teens/peer-pressure.html

Peer pressure or influence: pre-teens and teenagers. (n.d). Raising Children. https://raisingchildren.net.au/teens/behaviour/peers-friends-trends/peer-influence

Peterson, T.J. (2023, October 20). *Failure to launch syndrome: causes, therapy options, & 7 ways to cope.* Choosing therapy. https://www.choosingtherapy.com/failure-to-launch-syndrome/

Pickhardt, E, C. (2010, March 23). *Adolescence and the problem of parental expectations.* Psychology Today. https://www.psychologytoday.com/ca/blog/surviving-your-childs-adolescence/201003/adolescence-and-the-problem-parental-expectations

Pietrangelo, A. (2019, December 12). *9 CBT Techniques for better mental health.* Healthline. https://www.healthline.com/health/cbt-techniques

Positive and negative effects of peer pressure. (n.d). Sanjeev Datta. https://sanjeevdatta.com/effects-of-peer-pressure/

Quinn, D. (2022, December 26). *Cognitive Restructuring in CBT: Steps, techniques, & examples.* Sandstone Care. https://www.sandstonecare.com/blog/cognitive-restructuring-cbt/

Ramirez, L. (n.d). *Balance between digital and face-to-face friends.* Liberty University. https://www.liberty.edu/students/health-wellness/becoming-wellness-champions-blog/balance-between-digital-and-face-to-face-interactions/

Raypole, C. (2020, May 28). *5 visualization techniques to add to your meditation practice.* Healthline. https://www.healthline.com/health/visualization-meditation

Regan, S. (2021, December 11). *Struggle with self-love? Why you might want to look at yourself in the mirror.* MBG Mindfulness. https://www.mindbodygreen.com/articles/mirror-work

Rehman, A. (n.d). *The importance of goal setting in therapy.* Grief Recovery Center. https://www.griefrecoveryhouston.com/importance-of-goal-setting-in-therapy/

Reinicke, C. (2022, June 1). *54% of teenagers feel unprepared to finance their futures, survey shows.* CNBC. https://www.cnbc.com/2022/06/01/54percent-of-teens-feel-unprepared-to-finance-their-futures-survey-shows.html

Richardson, N. (2022, March 13). *How emotional intelligence builds resilience.*

The People Mentor. https://thepeoplementor.co.uk/how-emotional-intel
ligence-builds-resilience/

Rising parental expectations linked to perfectionism in college students. (2022,
March 31). American Psychology Association. https://www.apa.org/
news/press/releases/2022/03/parental-expectations-perfectionism

Robinson, L., Artley, A., Smith, M., Segal, J. (n.d). *Why are friends important?
Help Guide.* https://www.helpguide.org/articles/relationships-communica
tion/making-good-friends.htm

Robinson, L., Smith, M. (n.d). *Social media and mental health.* Help Guide.
https://www.helpguide.org/articles/mental-health/social-media-and-
mental-health.htm

Rodriguez, S, G. (n.d). *10 Surprising ways anxiety symptoms show up in the body.*
The Psychology Group. https://thepsychologygroup.com/10-surprising-
ways-anxiety-shows-up-in-the-body/

Romer, D. (2017, October 31). *The impulsive teen brain isn't based on science.*
Smithsonian Magazine. https://www.smithsonianmag.com/science-
nature/impulsive-teen-brain-not-based-science-180967027/

Romero, C. (2016, May 4). *Social media creates unrealistic life expectations.* Talon
Marks. https://www.talonmarks.com/opinion/2016/05/04/social-media-
creates-unrealistic-life-expectations/

Rubin, K,. Fredstrom, B,. Bowker, J. *Future directions in... Friendship in childhood
and early adolescence.* National Library of Medicine. https://www.ncbi.nlm.
nih.gov/pmc/articles/PMC5619663/

Sabater, V. (2023, March 24). *Socratic questioning for your limiting beliefs.*
Exploring Your Mind. https://exploringyourmind.com/socratic-question
ing-for-your-limiting-beliefs/

Salmansohn, K. (n.d). *Its not about how many friends you have.* Oprah. https://
www.oprah.com/spirit/friendship-is-about-quality-not-quantity/all

Saxena, S. (2023, October 4). *Peer pressure. Types, examples & how to respond.*
Choosing therapy. https://www.choosingtherapy.com/peer-pressure/

School stress: How student life affects your teen. (n.d). Embark Behavioral Health.
https://www.embarkbh.com/blog/school-stress/

Schweiser, S. (2020, February 27). *Coming of age in an age of uncertainty.* Bold.
https://bold.expert/coming-of-age-in-an-age-of-uncertainty/

Senior-year stress: Here's what students say and do about it. (n.d). College Data.
https://www.collegedata.com/resources/study-break/senior-year-stress

Self-confidence and teenagers. (n.d). Reach out. https://parents.au.reachout.com/skills-to-build/wellbeing/self-confidence-and-teenagers

Self esteem affirmations: building confidence in one's own worth. (n.d). Mather Hospital. https://www.matherhospital.org/weight-loss-matters/self-esteem-affirmations-building-confidence-in-ones-own-worth/

Self-monitoring. (n.d). Psychology Tools. https://www.psychologytools.com/professional/techniques/self-monitoring/

Shafir, H. (2022, December 13). *CBT for anxiety: How it works & examples.* Choosing Therapy. https://www.choosingtherapy.com/cbt-for-anxiety/

Siddhant, I. (2023, May 6). *The importance of positive affirmations.* LinkedIn. https://www.linkedin.com/pulse/importance-positive-affirmation-siddhant-iyer/

Sippi, A. (n.d). *7 cognitive flexibility strategies to support your adolescent.* Life Skills Advocate. https://lifeskillsadvocate.com/blog/7-flexible-thinking-strategies-to-support-your-teen-or-young-adult/

Sissons, B. (2023, September 19). *How to recognize and treat debilitating anxiety.* Medical News Today. https://www.medicalnewstoday.com/articles/debilitating-anxiety

60% of young people unable to cope due to pressure to succeed. (n.d). Mental Health Foundation. https://www.mentalhealth.org.uk/about-us/news/60-young-people-unable-cope-due-pressure-succeed

Smith, K. (2022, October 21). *6 common triggers of teen stress.* Psycom. https://www.psycom.net/common-triggers-teen-stress

Social media and risky behavior. (2023, October 6). Social Media Victims. https://socialmediavictims.org/effects-of-social-media/risky-behavior/

Social media's effect on self-esteem. (2023, September 18). Social Media Victims. https://socialmediavictims.org/mental-health/self-esteem/

Solomon, D. (n.d). *Social media has made beauty unattainable.* Next Generation Politics. https://www.nextgenpolitics.org/blog/social-media-beauty

Soza, S. (n.d). *School friendship issues: Your parent guide and teen workbook.* They Are The Future. https://www.theyarethefuture.co.uk/school-friendship-issues/

Stein. (n.d). *You've been lied to about anxiety: Why it gets worse when you try to feel better, and what you can do about it.* Effective Therapy Solutions. https://effectivetherapysolutions.com/anxiety/youve-been-lied-to-about-anxiety-why-it-gets-worse-when-you-try-to-feel-better-and-what-you-can-do-about-it

Stress and stress management: pre-teens and teenagers. (n.d). Raising Children. https://raisingchildren.net.au/pre-teens/mental-health-physical-health/ stress-anxiety-depression/stress-in-teens

Stress management and teens. (2019, January). American Academy of Child & Adolescent Society. https://www.aacap.org/AACAP/Families_and_Youth/ Facts_for_Families/FFF-Guide/Helping-Teenagers-With-Stress-066.aspx

Sutton, J. (2021, July 6). *How to perform assertiveness training: 6 exercises.* Positive Psychology. https://positivepsychology.com/assertiveness-training/

Teen Brain: Behavior, problem solving, and decision making. (2017, September). American Academy of Child & Adolescent Psychiatry. https://www.aacap. org/AACAP/Families_and_Youth/Facts_for_Families/FFF-Guide/The-Teen-Brain-Behavior-Problem-Solving-and-Decision-Making-095.aspx

Teen mental health : The importance of resilience in teens. (2023, March 9). MST Services. https://info.mstservices.com/blog/teen-mental-health-resilience

Teens: Relationship development. (n.d). Stanford Medicine. https://www.stan fordchildrens.org/en/topic/default?id=relationship-development-90-P01642

Telloian, C. (2022, July 29). *8 ways to become emotionally resilient.* Psych Central . https://psychcentral.com/health/tips-for-becoming-emotionally-resilient

10 forms of cyberbullying. (2015, October 27). Kids Safety by Kaspersky. https://kids.kaspersky.com/10-forms-of-cyberbullying/

10 limiting beliefs and how to overcome them. (2023. January 3). Asana. https:// asana.com/resources/limiting-beliefs

10 tips to manage time and tasks. (n.d). The University of Melbourne. https:// students.unimelb.edu.au/academic-skills/resources/learning-online/10-tips-to-manage-time-and-tasks

The adolescent brain: Beyond raging hormones. (2011, March 7). Harvard Health Publishing. https://www.health.harvard.edu/mind-and-mood/the-adoles cent-brain-beyond-raging-hormones

The advantages of cognitive behavioral therapy for teens. (n.d). Center for Child Development. https://thecenterforchilddevelopment.com/the-advan tages-of-cognitive-behavioral-therapy-for-teens/

The cognitive behavior therapy tools can help you manage stress. (2021, May 22). Goodnet. https://www.goodnet.org/articles/these-cognitive-behavior-therapy-tools-help-you-manage-stress

The importance of being present (and how to do it). (2020, October 30). Virtuagym.

https://business.virtuagym.com/magazine/the-importance-of-being-present-and-how-to-do-it/

The importance of self-worth. (n.d). Psych Alive. https://www.psychalive.org/self-worth/

The importance of teen friendships. (2022, June 13). Newport Academy. https://www.newportacademy.com/resources/empowering-teens/teen-friendships/

The surprising learning power of the mirror. (n.d), Love Every. https://lovevery.com/community/blog/child-development/the-surprising-learning-power-of-a-household-mirror/

Tips on how to grow your support system. (n.d). Essence of Healing Counseling. https://www.essenceofhealingcounseling.com/support-system/

Understanding anxiety in kids and teens. (n.d). Mass General Brigham Mclean. https://www.mcleanhospital.org/essential/anxiety-kids-teens

Understanding social comparison on social media. (n.d). The Jed Foundation. https://jedfoundation.org/resource/understanding-social-comparison-on-social-media/

Unlocking the power of a growth mindset: How Carol Dweck's research can help shape our children's future. (2023, April 21). Strobel Education. https://strobeleducation.com/blog/power-of-a-growth-mindset-carol-dwecks

Urdang, S. N. (2015, April 8). *Routines and rituals: Mindfulness as a tool for mastery.* Good Therapy. https://www.goodtherapy.org/blog/routines-and-rituals-mindfulness-as-a-tool-for-mastery-0408154

Using the cognitive triangle to combat anxiety and depression. (2017, April 10). SI News. https://www.sinews.es/en/using-the-cognitive-triangle-to-combat-anxiety-and-depression/

Using the mnemonic "three Cs" with children and adolescents. (2021, June 8). Beck Institute. https://beckinstitute.org/blog/using-the-mnemonic-three-cs-with-children-and-adolescents/

Vaes, J. (n.d). *Chain analysis: A powerful CBT tool to help you understand yourself.* Inner Path Seekers. https://theipsproject.com/2022/11/cbt-tool-to-help-you-understand-yourself/

Vallejo, M. *10 grounding exercises for kids to manage anxiety and worries.* (2022, November 14). Mental Health Center for Kids. https://mentalhealthcenterkids.com/blogs/articles/grounding-exercises-for-kids

Villines, Z. (2022, June 20). *Cognitive restructuring and its techniques.* Medical

News Today. https://www.medicalnewstoday.com/articles/cognitive-restructuring#role-in-cbt

Villines, Z. (2022, February 23). *What to know about peer pressure and drugs.* Medical News Today. https://www.medicalnewstoday.com/articles/peer-pressure-drugs

Well, T. (2020, January 2). *What the mirror can teach you about yourself: Advice from a mirror gazing expert.* Mindful. https://www.mindful.org/what-the-mirror-can-teach-you-about-yourself-advice-from-a-mirror-gazing-expert/

What is cognitive behavioral therapy (CBT)? (n.d). Anxiety Canada. https://www.anxietycanada.com/articles/what-is-cognitive-behaviour-therapy/

What are anxiety disorders? (n.d). American Psychiatric Association. https://www.psychiatry.org/patients-families/anxiety-disorders/what-are-anxiety-disorders

What are the effects of cyberbullying? (n.d). Kaspersky. https://www.kaspersky.com/resource-center/preemptive-safety/cyberbullying-effects#:

What are the six types of peer pressure? (n.d). Talk it Out. https://www.talkitoutnc.org/types-of-peer-pressure/

What is cognitive behavioral therapy? (n.d). APA. https://www.apa.org/ptsd-guideline/patients-and-families/cognitive-behavioral

What is mirror work? (n.d). Louise Hay. https://www.louisehay.com/what-is-mirror-work/

What to do when you over-commit. (n.d). Mother Nurture. https://www.themothernurture.com/blog/2023/4/19/what-to-do-when-you-over-commit

When does anxiety warrant professional help? (n.d). Plymouth Psycho Group. https://www.plymouthpsychgroup.com/blog/when-does-anxiety-warrant-professional-help

Why are teen friendships so important to mental health? (2021, February 25). Thrive Training and Consulting. https://www.thrivetrainingconsulting.com/why-are-teen-friendships-so-important-to-mental-health/

Why failure is healthy for teens. (2017, July 13). Newport Academy. https://create.dibbly.com/d/d5VZnLBsBT3KBvaiUb0q

Why self-worth matters, and how to improve it. (2023, October 25). Better Help. https://www.betterhelp.com/advice/self-esteem/why-self-worth-matters-and-how-to-improve-it/

Why teens drink and experiment with drugs. (n.d). Partnership to End Addiction.

https://drugfree.org/article/why-teens-drink-and-experiment-with-drugs/

Wong, B. (2023, May 18). *Top social media statistics and trends of 2023.* Forbes Advisor. https://www.forbes.com/advisor/business/social-media-statistics/

Yelishala, A. (2022, January 12). *The impact of social media on peer pressure in adolescents.* Youth Medical Journal. https://youthmedicaljournal.word press.com/2022/01/12/the-impact-of-social-media-on-peer-pressure-in-adolescents/

Zucker, B. (2021, November 26). *Using social media for reassurance and validation.* Psychology Today. https://www.psychologytoday.com/ca/blog/liber ate-yourself/202111/using-social-media-reassurance-and-validation

Made in United States
Troutdale, OR
12/20/2024